THE
EXECUTIVE'S
COMPETITIVE
EDGE

Why You Need to Leverage the Talents & Time of an Executive Assistant

By

Joan Burge

and

James Bristow

Published by Office Dynamics International
Las Vegas, NV

TESTIMONIALS

"*The Executive's Competitive Edge is full of insightful and practical advice for taking the relationship between the Executive and the Executive Assistant to a whole new level. I especially found the advice on building trust and effective delegation super inspiring – especially given all we have experienced during the pandemic. Joan and James do a wonderful job of describing the process of building this critical relationship from their unique perspective – so many executives I know would benefit from their coaching tips. I am fortunate to have an amazing Executive Assistant, who recommended the book to me. I am excited to work with her to continue to improve our relationship and impact on the business!*" **—Maureen Montgomery, Global Product Supply HR and Corporate Function, Procter & Gamble**

"*This outstanding book, distinguished by clarity of detail, will change the way we think about the Executive/Executive Assistant relationship and its contribution to business success. The authors have removed the ambiguity that continues to exist in how the Executive/ Executive Assistant business partnership is perceived. The Executive's Competitive Edge looks at the biases and misconceptions that affect how the Executive Assistant role is perceived and is instructive in revitalizing these careers. The challenge, opportunity, and clear advantage for the Executive is to reimagine the Executive Assistant role.*" **—Melba Duncan, President, The Duncan Group**

"Joan Burge and James Bristow have written a remarkable book that reveals the secrets of building a strategic partnership between an executive and executive assistant. Along the way, they dispel myths about the roles and cast a vision for what today's Exec/EA partnership is capable of becoming. If you're looking for a guide full of insightful and savvy best practices, this book is an essential read!"
—Don Harms, Founder /CEO of Emmre

"I love how this book provides guidance, and real-world scenarios on the importance of the executive and executive assistant's business partnership. Having a strong EA has benefited me in so many ways. There are so many ways my EA enhances my life both professionally and personally, and I could not have the efficiency and peace of mind if I did not have the business partnership we have in place. This book is definitely a relevant read for any executive or executive assistant looking to build a successful partnership together." **—Karen Walker, SVP & Chief Marketing Officer, Intel Corporation**

"An excellent EA as a productivity hack is not something I've considered previously. Coming from the tech space, I have always found comfort in "there's an app for that." In reality, I have spent countless hours researching, learning, and maintaining my "productivity tools." Throughout The Executive's Competitive Edge, Joan and James give multi-generational examples of how the EA role has evolved from screening calls and booking travel to having a true strategic partner; an extension of yourself who allows you to focus on the mission-critical tasks of a business leader. If you've been putting off hiring an executive assistant, this book makes a powerful argument to make it a priority." **—Brad Johnson, Startup Executive/Entrepreneur**

"The Executive's Competitive Edge is a captive dialogue between two professional leaders who have truly mastered the art of executive delegation, which most leaders struggle to perfect. In mastering this skill, Joan and James have successfully harmonized the coexistence of work, life, and family." —**Brian Kirkpatrick, President Universal Engineering Sciences**

"What executive can resist a competitive edge? The conversational style of these two authors sharing their individual expertise makes this book an easy and quick read for the busy executive! It is engagingly informative and even entertaining. Go hire an executive assistant and use this book as a roadmap to success creating even more time, productivity, revenue and partnership in your life and business!" —**Angelina Galindo, Business Coach, Galindo Group**

"There could be no better time for Joan Burge's new book, The Executive's Competitive Edge than now. There could be no better person to co-author this book than Joan Burge. My own career spans four decades of consulting and search in the executive support specialty area. This book will illuminate, educate, inspire executives to understand the exponential leveraging of focus, productivity and success that is available for those who partner with the right Executive Assistant. They will learn why and how it is possible. I highly recommend The Executive's Competitive Edge as a 'must read' for leaders who want to change and grow... their capacity and their achievement." —**Leni Miller, President, EASearch, LLC**

"Joan Burge is a tour de force in the world of business and Executive Assistants. Her new book The Executive's Competitive EDGE strikes at the immense value and importance of this role. A must read for Executives and EAs alike!" —**Daren Martin, PhD, The Culture Architect, Global Speaker, and Author**

"The Executive's Competitive Edge is a must read for executives to better understand and utilize the skills of their executive assistants and how executive assistants can take their expertise to the next level. Starting my career as an executive assistant and now as an executive, I know firsthand the importance of creating a team on both sides. And Joan Burge and James Bristow define the true meaning of team building through their own experiences. This insightful information provides good practical advice and "gems" for up and coming as well as experienced executives and executive assistants." —**Teresa Peters, President, Stanton Partners**

"A clear outline on the power of the Executive Assistant and a clear representation on how to make this partnership work. I have had an amazing experience in working with my Executive Assistant partner for the last 10 years. This book is a great roadmap to not only building that partnership but to look at the partnership in new and powerful ways. A strong Executive Assistant can be a clear game changer in an executive's success. Investing time in making this work is time well spent." —**Maurice DuPas, VP Customer Experience, Cisco Systems**

TABLE OF CONTENTS

A Message of Thanks to Our Strategic Partners 12

A Note to Readers Regarding Titles and Gender 14

A Personal Note From Joan Burge 15

Introduction: Why This Book and Why Now 17

Part 1: Why You Need an Executive Assistant 23

Myths, Myths, and More Myths 24

Your Direct Reports Are Different From an Executive Assistant 26

You Need an Accountability Partner 26

It Is Lonely at the Top 30

I Have To Bite My Tongue 32

New Risks 32

Executive Assistants Are Influential 36

The Calm in the Storm 42

Soften the Blow 43

Well-Connected 46

An Extension of You 47

Relieve Executive's Decision Fatigue 48

Point Out Your Blind Spots 49

Just Because You Can, Does Not Mean You Should 52

A Word About Personal Assistants 57

The Challenge of a Virtual Setting 58

Addressing the Elephant in the Room 60

Mission Critical Challenge 61

Your Competitive Edge 62

Joan's Caveat: There Is No Magic 66

Gems To Lead By 67

Part 2: Tectonic Shifts **69**

A Very Personal Story 70

The Hybrid Workplace 74

The Evolving Role of the Executive 76

The Future-Minded Leader 77

The Need for Speed 78

The World Is Getting Much Smaller 79

The Great Resignation 80

Heavily Trimmed Executive Assistant Staff 81

Virtual Meeting Burnout 82

The World Is a Lot Less Personal 83

Why is Working in the Office So Beneficial to Business? 86

The Evolving Assistant 89

Blending of Your Personal and Professional Life 90

Your Competitive Edge 91

Gems To Lead By 93

Part 3: Building A Strategic Partnership **95**

The Three Stages of an Executive/EA Pairing 96

The Foundation for a Successful Partnership 99

How To Create a Strategic Partnership 100

Being in Agreement 101

Define the Goals of the Partnership 102

Define the Role(s) of Each Partner 102

Identify Advantageous Behaviors 103

Remember: You Are Both Human 103

Genuinely Care 104

Value and Respect Each Other 105

Build Exceptional Levels of Trust 105

Be Willing To Have Uncomfortable Conversations 105

Realize You Are Dependent on Each Other 106
To Achieve Results

Communicate, Communicate, Communicate! 107

Model Other Great Leaders 108

Become Champions of Change 109

Your Competitive Edge 111

Gems To Lead By 113

Part 4: How to Maximize the Time **115**
and Talents of an Executive Assistant

Benefits of Leveraging Your Executive Assistant's Skills 116

Changing Perceptions 117

The Executive Assistant as an Information Flow Manager 119

Blending Both Worlds 121

The Art of Delegation 123

Barriers to Delegation 123

Delegate More 124

The Benefits of Delegating 126

Delegation Requires Trust 129

Deciding Which Tasks To Assign to Your 132
Executive Assistant

Discuss Task Expectations 146

Release Slowly 146

The Value of Human Moments 152

Putting It All Together: The Maximized 165
Executive Assistant

Executive Assistant Talent: Tech Leader   168

Executive Assistant Talent: Moves Mountains   172

Allow Your Executive Assistant To Own Something   173
They Are Passionate About

Inclusion   175

     Meetings   176

     Belonging   179

Avoid Micro-Managing   179

Your Assistant Has Needs Too   182

Your Competitive Edge   185

Gems To Lead By   188

Part 5: Why You Need To Invest in Professional Development   **189**

Learning in Tandem Leads to Growing in Tandem   190

Your Executive Assistant Must Optimize Current Skills   195
and Learn New Skills

     Unceasing Change   195

     Molding Their Career   195

     Competitive Marketplace   195

     Pace at Which We Work   196

     Senior Executives Have Higher Expectations   196
     of Administrative Staff

     Build Confidence   196

     Personal Satisfaction Leading to Happier Lives   196

Be a Catalyst for Cultural Change   197

How To Support Your Executive Assistant's Development   197

What Kind of Training Does Your Executive Assistant Need?   200

Coaching for You, the Executive   202

Your Competitive Edge   203

Gems To Lead By   205

Part 6: Looking for a Star Performer   **207**

Not Just Anyone Can Be a Stellar Executive Assistant!   208

The DNA of a Star Assistant 209

The Interview: What To Look for; What To Run From 210

    Before the Interview 211

    Skills 212

    Attitudes/Traits/Behaviors 212

    During the Interview 213

    Situational/Behavioral 213

    Skills 214

    Traits 215

    Follow-up Interviews 217

    Stay Away From 217

You are Hired! 218

Need an EA Search Firm? 218

Your Competitive Edge 220

Joan's Final Word to Executives 221

Appendix **223**

    Additional Resources 224

    Books by Joan Burge 225

    About the Authors 226

A MESSAGE OF THANKS TO OUR STRATEGIC PARTNERS

Melia Amira started with Office Dynamics in 2006 as an Administrative Assistant to my then-Chief Executive Assistant and me. Upon the amicable departure of my CEA, Melia stepped in to become my Executive Assistant and evolved into my strategic partner.

Melia, thank you so much for the times you have "talked me down off the ledge," held me accountable for my action items, made me laugh, dealt with my last-minute creative ideas, been my sounding board, returned numerous Cruella Halloween outfits and wigs (LOL), all the while exhibiting constant calmness. It is not easy to be the Executive Assistant to the global leader in the administrative training industry.

I must also thank Jasmine Freeman, my former Chief Executive Assistant, who stood by my side for ten years; the most difficult ten years of my life. Together we weathered my husband's cancer battle (which he lost), my brain surgery, my open-heart surgery, and several economic storms. You handled all those situations with style, grace, professionalism, and utmost privacy. I am so grateful we remain good friends.

Joan Burge
CEO and Founder
Office Dynamics International

A special thank you to Ms. Kayla Hutchens for teaching me to be a better leader. By showing me her understanding and her commitment, she has allowed me to become more understanding and committed myself. Trust, communication, and compassion are the tenants of our relationship, and if and when one of those tenants isn't working right, it is almost ALWAYS my fault. Thank you, Kayla, for never holding that against me. Thank you for being you and for all that you do.

Also, thank you to my previous Executive Assistants, the other Executive Assistants within our organization, and to the Executive Assistants that I have worked with outside of our business. Without each of you, simply put, I would not be who I am today, nor would I be able to see clearly who I want to be in the future. For the sake of focused recognition—thank you to Amanda Glaeser and Carolyn Chalupka-Pope—you each demonstrate and embody the power of strategic partnership in your roles as EAs for influential partners in my life, and for that, I am grateful.

James Bristow
Managing Partner
Universal Engineering Sciences

A NOTE TO READERS REGARDING TITLES AND GENDER

For purposes of consistency and inclusion, in this book we have chosen to use the following terminology:

Titles:

- There are more than 100 titles under the administrative profession umbrella. In this book we will use the title "Executive Assistant" also abbreviated as "EA," for all such positions.

- There are many titles designating the person in charge, including executive, leader, entrepreneur, manager, business owner, or other specific C-Suite positions. In this book we will use the title "Executive" for all such positions.

Gender:

- Though women still comprise the majority of administrative professionals, in this book we will use gender-neutral language to respect all members of the profession and to acknowledge the evolving demographics.

A PERSONAL NOTE FROM JOAN BURGE

DEAR EXECUTIVE,

As of this writing, I have been in the business world 52 years. I spent the first 20 years as an Executive Assistant. During that time, I worked in 12 different companies in five states. These relocations were not because I performed poorly. The reason for all the moves was because I was an eager, hungry EA who wanted to achieve the highest levels within my profession. Or, if I was not happy at a company or job, I departed. I always believed I needed to like where I spent 40+ hours a week. Other job transitions occurred because two employers downsized and in each, my position was cut; other changes were because I moved out of state with my husband, who kept excelling in his career.

Eventually I realized that I wanted to do something different but did not know what. Being an EA was the only occupation I knew, and it was a career I loved. Eventually, I realized there was a huge gap between the ongoing training and development my Executives received and the career-specific training I got—which was basically none! It made no sense to me that my Executives were afforded multiple opportunities to professionally develop and I, the person running their lives, got nothing.

In 1990, I started Office Dynamics (renamed "Office Dynamics International" in 2012), dedicating myself to creating and teaching robust administrative career-specific courses, workshops, conferences, and coaching, as well as authoring several books[1]. This work ultimately led me to coaching CEOs, Executives, and business owners on how to work more effectively with their EAs and how to build strategic partnerships with them. I have been an Executive, business owner, and CEO for over 32 years, so I know what things look like from your side of the desk.

I can honestly tell you from all this experience in the business world there is no greater, more vital relationship in the workplace than that of an Executive and their Executive Assistant. When these two people come together as strategic partners, they can move mountains, change the corporate culture, and help shape the world.

I sincerely hope you will read this book with an open mind as my co-author, James Bristow, and I share our different perspectives leading you to the same outcomes. Our purpose is to encourage you to:

- Hire an EA if you do not have one.
- If you have an EA, maximize their talents and time.
- Encourage your colleagues to retain and leverage an EA.
- Champion and talk about the value these EAs bring to your organization.

Wishing you much success!

Joan

---

[1] See Appendix for a list of books authored by Joan Burge.

INTRODUCTION

WHY THIS BOOK, AND WHY NOW?

Put simply ... Life and work are complicated.
The world has dramatically changed.
The stakes have never been higher!

How Joan and James Met

JAMES: *Joan and I met in an internationally recognized CEO Peer Advisory Group, where we each participated to advance our skills for increasing value and reducing risk in our respective business. I served as a founding member for the new group inside an existing national network because I was looking for a peer group where good minds could gather to support each other and be led by a Chair that would awaken any hidden energies. I found that the energies were in fact awakened by the other members of the group in addition to the Chair, and one such energetic soul was Joan. She has proven to be a special friend and partner, in business and now, in life.*

One of my favorite aspects of the relationship that Joan and I have is that she is a young soul and an older woman, while I am an old soul and younger man; between this dichotomy lies the creative solutions and opinions that we have developed for this book and many of the initiatives we collaborate on for our professional roles in our businesses. Our minds work very differently, and it is in that diversity of thought where the power truly lies. We have learned to challenge each other and poke at the assumptions and understanding of the world that each of us believe to be truth. Most importantly though, we find that without our EA strategic partners, we cannot work at our highest level, and together, we decided to share this multi-generational perspective with as many people as we could.

James Chooses Office Dynamics International

Joan and James' meeting through the CEO Peer Advisory Group eventually led James to send his firm's Executive Assistants to Office Dynamics International's (ODI) training courses and administrative conferences.

JAMES: *ODI's training was something I could support to demonstrate the investment in my administrative team members and to "really put my money where my mouth was." Other team members had received training but not this group. We were searching for this prior to my meeting Joan.*

For engineering, which is the main business that I'm in, the career path takes you through an undergraduate education. Once you graduate, most engineers have additional studies for a graduate-level degree. All our engineers, scientists, and engineering technicians have continuing education and professional development opportunities, but we could not find a way to push our administrative staff forward concurrently. I was looking for something that showed we cared about our administrative staff as well, and we were not just saying we cared but found a way to prove it. ODI created that opportunity.

When I met Joan and she introduced me to the curriculum created by ODI, it was fortuitous to find this great set of programs that catered to a variety of learning experiences for this under-served part of our team.

An Executive Who "Gets It"

JOAN: *I joined Vistage Las Vegas as I wanted to be in a CEO peer group that understood the challenges I had as a CEO and business owner. I wanted to interact with a group of diversified individuals who could shed a different perspective on my thinking and who would challenge my thinking, poke holes in it, and help me to make uncomfortable decisions. Our group was quite eclectic, representing various industries and a range of ages, with me being the eldest person in the group.*

I was impressed with James Bristow from the first meeting. James was a young, sharp Executive who owned his own business. He was a brilliant engineer and businessperson, yet down-to-earth and friendly. James was a leader in our group and a mentor to all, including me.

I was highly impressed that James "got it" when it came to his Executive Assistant. Many of our group's members did not enlist Executive Assistants, although they certainly could have benefited from having an EA. James knew this was a power position with great value. James saw and treated his Executive Assistant as a partner. He wanted to invest in his Executive Assistant's education through attending our conferences and certification courses.

The Book Idea

JOAN: *James initiated the idea of our collaborating on a book to tell Executives why they need to leverage an Executive Assistant and how to fully utilize their time and talents. In 2021, we met for lunch with our own Executive Assistants to float ideas and concepts for the book. We departed our lunch confident in the knowledge we had an important message to deliver to the world of Executives. From there, we set our wheels in motion, and the result is now in your hands.*

JAMES: *I read 40 – 50 books a year. There are so many books that were written to me as a leader, CEO, or business owner about how to do this, or the top ten ways to do that, or tips and tricks on how to be a better Executive. They were all about leadership, but none seemed to really get into the weeds about how to be effective and get things done. These books were valuable in their own way, but I have boiled them all down to the conclusion that I'm nothing without strong people and a supportive team. And one of the most crucial team members in a highly effective team is a strong and skillful Executive Assistant.*

I believe that servant leadership, which is how I like to lead, is most effective if I spend the majority of my time personally interacting with team members and clients. I cannot do that if I'm making PowerPoint presentations, booking my own travel, or scheduling my own calendar. Before I found the power of an Executive Assistant, I kept thinking about the amount of time I was using that DID NOT put me in front of the people I needed to serve. Then, it hit me. I needed someone who believes in servant leadership and aims to effectuate this leadership by serving the leader as a critical division of the Executive's Office. I wish someone would have told me much sooner that with a great Executive

Assistant, I could reach and serve more people. With an Executive Assistant who grows into a Strategic Partner, I could **exponentially** *increase impact. The fact that I wanted somebody in hindsight to tell me that story and tell me sooner, led me to want to share this with other Executives.*

Age 37 Meets 69 and Goals Are Established

At the writing of this book, James is 37 and Joan is 69. They thought it would be great to team together on this book to share different generational viewpoints and that some things never change—there is a just a new twist.

JAMES: *Joan might do something that I would say is old school, but then she will do something new school, and it will catch me off guard and I love that. I would like to say I'm an old soul, but I'm kind of new school. I will do something that's old school and Joan finds it refreshing and comfortable. What it proves to me is that there is the ability to bridge those generational differences.*

Maybe we don't need to change some of the old ways or thought processes just for the sake of change. There are certain things from the generations and decades before me that simply just make sense. However, maybe there is a new or different tool to get things done. I like to challenge Joan to think about change in a positive light. A basic example is that I should not be allowed to touch my calendar, but there are great digital collaboration tools for my EA and I to share for calendar management.

We also have writing stylistic differences that are not related to age, but rather, style preferences.

James' writing style is largely analytical and black and white. He writes from the vantage point of a highly educated and credentialed leader in an established and well-regulated industry. His writing balances his extensive thought leadership with an unabashed openness to share real-world experience about how to best manage the Executive/EA strategic partnership and how and when issues can be mitigated in a frank yet kind manner. His overarching principle is "operate with kindness, first and always."

Joan's writing style is pointed and brief, yet passionate and well-researched. She knows her industry well and is a respected leader within that community. Her writing is meant to educate and motivate anyone in, around, or related to the administrative profession —whether an Executive, HR business partner, or an EA. Her overarching principle is "keep growing and give your very best to anything you do."

We hope that these style differences will keep you engaged while reading the book!

Our goals for this book and for you are to:
- *Show you why you need an Executive Assistant.*
- *Teach you how to leverage the time and talent of an Executive Assistant (whether you have a new relationship or an established relationship).*
- *Merge best practices from both generations.*
- *Help up-and-coming Executives see how to bridge timeless success practices with new-world thought.*
- *Establish a mindset that allows your Executive Assistant to grow into your strategic business partner.*

WHY YOU NEED AN EXECUTIVE ASSISTANT

Have you heard, thought, or said any of the following statements?

"Why do I need an Executive Assistant? I can manage my own calendar, emails, travel, and much more. If I have an EA, I will just have to take time to explain things. And it is not cost effective to have an extra person on the payroll expense line."

"Surely the department EA can support five leaders with very busy schedules. After all, anyone can do that job."

"We will create a centralized pool for assistants, and each will take a piece of a project based on their skill level. It will save time."

"Assistants are replaceable."

"When a crisis hits the organization, let go of the EAs first. They really are not necessary."

"I am an Executive and I do not need an Executive Assistant to help me. It shows weakness if I ask for help and I cannot appear weak to my team!"

Myths, Myths, and More Myths

These statements are myths and clearly show that individual contributors, managers, leaders, and HR professionals may not really understand the role of an Executive Assistant. They do not comprehend the full breadth and depth of what goes on behind the scenes or understand the complexity of an Executive's schedule, relationships, and initiatives. They do not see the hours an EA spends changing 20 meetings five times in two weeks. Or see the EA trying to sift through 250+ emails a day.

You Do Not Mess With the Sentry

Former Humana CEO, Mike McCallister, told Joan Burge in an interview that his EA was his flow manager. His EA had the ability to let people in to see him, or, if she did not like you, somehow there was no room on the calendar for you.

The CEO said his EA had more power than most people realized. Mike was so convinced about the power of the profession that under his leadership, Humana spent over ten years training their assistants to operate at the top of their game and to prepare them for future positions with greater responsibility.

JOAN: *When I was an EA, I had power. I had the unspoken authority to let people through or not; to make someone's life easier or not; to loosen bottlenecks or create barriers. I had a hidden power. EAs might be "behind the scenes," but their presence makes a difference. They can create a powerful ripple effect through the organization. Most often, they want things to move quickly, easily, and efficiently ... and they have the power to do that!*

JOAN: *I know the administrative job inside and out based on my experiences and from training and interacting with tens of thousands of assistants globally. I intimately know what it takes to be successful in this role, including the breadth and depth of skills needed for a great Executive/EA relationship to work. The role is* *so much bigger than what most people perceive. You will see that as you read this book.*

Your Direct Reports Are Different From an Executive Assistant

JOAN: *Over three decades some Executives have told me, "I do not see the difference between an EA and my direct reports." Well, your direct reports are not running your life! There are times they will not and cannot act as your sounding board. They are not your 100% confidante like your EA can be. A great EA will watch your back and look down the rails for oncoming trains like no one else in the organization will do for you. The relationship between an Executive and their EA is unique.*

EAs Describe Themselves

- Enable my Executive to do their best work.
- Run after complex problems.
- Strategically deploy my Executive's time.
- Growth accelerator.
- Creative problem solver.
- Opportunity identifier.
- Offshoot of my Executive's brand.
- Master facilitator of my Executive's time.
- Calm under pressure.

You Need an Accountability Partner

JAMES: *Granted I was not alive then, but from what I can tell, a 1950s-era high-performing, fast-paced Executive did not worry about* *what was on his or her calendar. A great EA would screen visitors and phone calls, transmit messages, advise the Executive when and where to go, and remove barriers in front of the Executive so they could work at the top of their licensure[2]. As far as I can tell, there is no reason for this effectiveness to change 70 years later, or ever.*

On the traditional organizational chart, you have an EA function that is placed off to the side of the Executive and it appears to be floating in space—this EA is out there and that is where it has just always sat. The traditional organization chart has started to evolve; we now have the evolution of the Chief of Staff position that floats in a similar space and may even overlap partially in functionality. You may have one or the other of these roles, or perhaps even have both a Chief of Staff and an Executive Assistant because their functions can be defined separately. You could also put them together and simply title your EA as the Chief of Staff if their role requires some additional C-suite responsibilities.

If your organization does not allow for EAs, they may allow for a Chief of Staff if they have duties that are more strategic or Executive in nature. I love the term Joan uses — strategic business partner. I consider both my Chief of Staff and my EA as strategic business partners. My Chief of Staff is an actual equity partner in a few of the legal entities that we manage, while I introduce my EA as my strategic business partner all the time. There is no better compliment that I can give Kayla.

I always talk about trying to live a blended lifestyle rather than a balanced lifestyle. It has become more difficult to be balanced, and

---

[2] *"Working at the top of licensure" means putting your mind and time to the highest possible use in diagnosing issues, successfully completing corporate initiatives, providing thought leadership, and quality client care — doing those things that your training has prepared you for, and enabling support staff to handle everything else.*

frankly, when I tried to balance my life, I only became more stressed out. I found that the more I focused on trying to be balanced the less likely I could do it and the more frustrated I got. I have young children. I have a significant other. I have a house, dogs, gymnastics practice, choir performances, track meets, and book reports. On top of loving my partner and children, I have other personal passions which include continued education, engineering research, professional relationships, community service, and my work and leadership within the engineering and construction markets.

Sharing that initiative or lifestyle desire with my EA strategic partner gave permission to help encourage it to flourish. My EA will say, "By the way, you are going to be in Orlando on Friday. Why don't you make a weekend out of it with the family and stay Saturday and Sunday to do Disney stuff? Then, on the flight back, I have calendared time for you to work on your current research paper since that journal deadline is coming up next month." That blending is super powerful and, most importantly, removes the stress of trying to balance something that changes by the minute.

For "old school" Executives, this mindset may be unnerving but with the integration of cell phones, laptops, and other technological tools into our daily business lives, we should have increased mobility and connectivity. Ironically, this increased connectivity makes balance EVEN HARDER to maintain. Any Executives who are struggling to balance work, home, self, health and feel like it is getting harder to do by the day, you are not alone. It is getting harder. You will find that when you stop trying to balance, you will enjoy a peaceful blend. You can let your EA help manage balancing your time with your initiatives, as they are most capable of understanding the logistics of your life.

My generation is connected to the world in real time, so trying to compartmentalize just does not work anymore. It causes more chaos and stress than it is worth. I have buddies that carry two cell phones because they have their work phone and their personal phone. Unless there is a security reason, why would you intentionally create inefficiency in your life? They end up using both cell phones for everything, forget which one is for what purpose and ultimately, drop one of them off the side of the fishing boat when trying to reel in a bluefin tuna (true story).

Joan's BIG Life 5 Pillars:

JOAN: *In 2012, I authored a book, Give Yourself Permission to Live a BIG Life. This was a year after my husband, Dave, died of pancreatic cancer (at the age of 60) after three years of battling the ugly disease. Dave and I juggled careers, children, grandchildren, family crises, and life. In that book, I gave birth to the idea to stop saying "life balance." Instead, I suggested you give equal attention, over a year's time, to the 5 Pillars: Career, Family, Financial, Spiritual, and Wellness.*

I had found that my Pillars were never in balance and that was an unrealistic, stressful way to live. Sometimes Career needs more attention. Sometimes Family takes center stage. Other times, bad health gets in the way.

Many organizations are using the words "integration" or "blending." Personally, I still like being business focused Monday – Friday, 8 a.m. – 5 p.m., but I have definitely flexed to leave at 4:00 p.m. to exercise or leave the office early on a Friday. Of course, I think about business outside typical business hours as well. When I am in my "business-thinking" mode, I do not like being interrupted with personal stuff. I like to stay in my "zone" for better flow and increased productivity.

Fortunately, I am at a stage in life and in my business where I have more flexibility in my day-to-day. I am a little unusual in that the word "retirement" is not in my vocabulary. I do not have a stop-date. I love my work, which is helping others be their professional and personal best. My work feeds my soul, gives me energy (most of the time), and keeps me challenged mentally. I fully subscribe to paying attention to my 5 Pillars.

It Is Lonely at the Top

JAMES: *Civil engineers have to work for a certain number of professional engineers for a certain period of time before they get their own licensure. It is a very formal process that we jokingly liken to indentured servitude. As I was in pursuit of licensure, I worked for a number of professional engineers, but just one served as a true mentor. I learned many things from him, and I always say that I learned a bit of what to do from him and a bit of what not to do from him. He laughs and nods when I tell him the same.*

One of the most important things that my mentor shared with me as I was growing in the management team was a lesson about what it means to be at the top. He told me, "You cannot complain downward in the organization. You can only complain upward." How challenging is that spot if you cannot complain down? It is lonely at the top.

An example of a lonely time I experienced as an Executive came when we owned our own engineering firm, called NOVA, where I served as the CEO and Managing Partner. It was during my tenure at NOVA (this entity was born out of the firm I worked for with the mentor mentioned) that I sought to join a CEO peer advisory group to create a sort of Board of Directors. In 2019, my partners and I determined that we needed to recapitalize to stabilize the organization and to breathe new life into it. From May 2019 to May 2020, I worked day and night on the sale of the business, having to quarterback our team through financial preparedness, Confidential Information Memoranda, investment banker meetings, interviews with prospective partners, LONG legal structure and agreement conversations, and the like. During this time, I had seven partners in NOVA and if it were not for those partners and the conversations that we had, I would have gone crazy, completely bonkers. But even with those partners, there were things that I could not say that I could tell my EA.

It was my way to create a sounding board, a whiteboard session, a mind dump, or just a straight up good old-fashioned complaining session. I would say to my EA, "Look, I have permission to have some of your time, yes? I am going to tell you some stuff and I do not need you to say anything. I do not need a solution. I just need to say it out loud for my sanity. And when I am done, I am going to go back to my desk and get back to work." It is so therapeutic. What a blessing to have somebody who can handle that. And that stuff is not easy to handle sometimes. Most Executives do not want to carry that weight home and for most, it is unhealthy to share the really heavy stuff with family since they usually don't have context or foundational understanding to handle it. If you can have that release during the day with someone in the organization, how much better are you going to be when you go home?

I Have To Bite My Tongue

JOAN: *As a professional speaker, business owner, and CEO, I cannot always say what I want to say. I need to be tactful and professional. The problem is other people are not very tactful in their communications. I can vent to my EA about how I really feel. Then my EA will cushion my message, or she will craft her own message in a way that gets the message across, yet saves face. Who is your sounding board? Who, at work, will listen to you rant and rave without judgment? Who will soften your message? Or be your day-to-day spokesperson?*

New Risks

JAMES: *I have been in the same business for 20 years and it has changed quite a bit over that time. I always say this is the only job I have ever had, but I have had every job in the business. Aside from the obvious changes, like our company name, the capitalization structure, our size and complexity, technology implementation, etc., the business "go to market" strategies and the risks associated with the industry have changed. Many of these risks are industry agnostic and Executives have many things to be concerned with in their day-to-day operations; these risks may be employment practice liabilities, such as stringent labor laws, evolving DEIB (diversity, equity, inclusion, and belonging) principles, COVID-19 management, prevention of hostile work environments, and more, but also include financial risks within volatile supply chains, inflationary labor costs, and staffing issues caused by the Great Resignation. With all of these stresses on the businesses and Executives, it is proving harder and harder to develop and maintain* *human connections with the people in the businesses while effectively managing the risks. Further, with the adaptation of technology, there are geotagged videos, filtered photos, and social media blasts that influence perception and risk now, whereas a Polaroid slipping into the wrong hands was the extent of concern in that arena 30 years ago.*

The EA and Executive relationship can really address risk mitigation concerns. The more you lean into your EA or the more the EA leans into the Executive to show that support and care, that humanistic element is reinforced, so that focus on addressing all the "people side" of our organizations can develop.

JOAN'S STORY: *In 2014, I was diagnosed with a massive, rare skull-based brain tumor called a clival chordoma. I had not known this tumor was growing until July 4, 2014, when I woke up with painful headaches, weakness, and dry heaves. I was immediately rushed to the local emergency room. Later that night I found out about the tumor. My story is too long to tell here. I can tell you that if it was not for my at-that-time strategic partner, Jasmine Freeman, Office Dynamics could have been drastically affected. I was the business! I was the brand, the creator, visionary, instructional designer, trainer, speaker, and author. We did have other trainers, but most of our clients wanted me. Talk about risk!*

Jasmine Freeman jumped right in. She had to immediately assess our situation and handle all communications on behalf of the company and me without divulging my very private situation. This was no easy task. Plus, Jasmine was very worried about me. But because we had been building our partnership for years and Jasmine had grown in her role, she handled it with calm and grace and the support of other team members. (FYI: my 13-hour surgery was successful, and I am happy to report I have had clean brain scans ever since.)

Melia Amira Shines During Pandemic

JOAN: *At this writing, Melia Amira has been my strategic partner for almost six years. Melia was by my side, running the ball down the field, when the pandemic struck. 2020 was Office Dynamics' 30th year anniversary. I was supposed to travel to several cities and speak to assistants, we were hosting a three-day course in ten cities, hosting our Annual Conference for Administrative Excellence in October, and had many other celebratory events planned. I also had some big contracts with major corporations to go to their offices to train their assistants—all in person!*

We had a huge mess on our hands with in-person events, which required having to guarantee sums of money to hotels, whether people showed up or not. It was an extremely trying, stressful time. All our client contracts for onsite training were cancelled. Our in-person conference was in jeopardy and by late summer we pivoted the entire event to a live virtual event. Melia had to negotiate with every hotel where we had contracts. Melia had to communicate with hundreds of assistants who had registered for our public courses and our conferences. The list goes on and on.

Had Melia and I not grown a business partnership, she would not have been able to help at the level she did when the crisis hit. Do you have that kind of a partner? If not, why not?

Those are the types of things an EA strategic partner will do for you! Not just any assistant can deal with crises. And this is where that building the partnership along the way becomes critical. That is why you must delegate, get your EA in the business, tell your EA why you make the decisions you make so when they face a similar situation, they know how you would approach it, or they know who to go to for sound advice. My EA even knows who my attorney is and who manages my financials and investments.

JAMES: *Quite frankly, I believe that a good business does not need a strong Executive until there is a crisis. So not only is it the EA's shining moment when there is a crisis, but it could be the Executive's as well. As an Executive, it should be that you are there for the 5% of the days when something is going wrong. I say that God gave me strong shoulders for a reason … it is to carry the weights of the world so that others do not have to, and I find that the businesses that I lead rely on me during those times when the weight is too much for the operation only. I find that when I can step in to help carry the burden during a crisis, the organization responds very well. Not only is it helpful in that moment, but it also increases the potency and efficacy of my leadership with the team members. I think, "That's what they keep me around for." I have this sense of purpose and sense of meaning because a good well-oiled business does not need me to be here most days. I should be outgrowing the business or building strategic partnerships and alliances with other business leaders. But those times when you are really needed, you are needed at your best. And you are not at your best without your EA partner by your side; right there, ready to rock and roll; in front leading, or blocking, or right behind you for the lateral pass to take the ball and run with it! That is when an Executive and EA shine the most and the relationship flourishes. It is because the trust is built so quickly when things are going not so right.*

Executive Assistants Are Influential

JAMES: *The Executive Assistant is an expansion of the Executive's influence. When I view my influence in the world, I think I can have something like 20 very meaningful relationships, but my EA can have exponentially more impact because Kayla gets to capture my 20 meaningful relationships via me as a proxy and she gets to expand on each one of those relationships with her own relationships. The way I look at it in terms of sheer mathematics is:*

$$James'\ impact\ without\ EA:\ 20^1 = 20$$

$$James'\ impact\ with\ EA:\ 20^2 = 20\ x\ 20 = 400$$

This truly provides the Executive with a Competitive Edge! The meaningfulness of each of those relationships may be diluted to some degree because no one can effectively manage 400 relationships. However, by Kayla capturing my small sphere of influence and using her role in an exponential format, she can make my own influence grow. I find that allowing and encouraging the EA to manage their own relationships will facilitate them to create even more impact than perhaps that of the Executive alone. I find that the EA's influence really moves the needle.

JOAN: *My thoughts immediately go to internal influence. When I was an EA, I influenced:*
- *My Executives to change their minds (in a good way).*
- *The creation of new processes.*
- *Training for our company's Executive Assistants.*
- *Other Administrative Assistants in how to excel.*
- *Vendors to provide our company with cost-effective pricing.*

- *Updating my job title and salary.*
- *Who got to see my Executive without an appointment.*
- *Future Executives to have daily huddles with me.*
- *Expanding my role as an EA.*
- *Copy room staff to immediately process a last-minute print job for my Executive's retreat (we did not have soft copies then).*
- *Requesting our company cafeteria to prepare a custom lunch for my Executive because he was too busy to leave his office.*

I recognize not all EAs have that level of influence. I was influential because of how I treated others—with utmost respect, my cheerful personality, good attitude, knowing how to effectively communicate with others—and I had built good relationships with each person I met, and by adding a dash of assertiveness.

JAMES: *There are finite segmentations between internal and external influence. When I hear influence, initially, my brain goes external. I am a people person. In my efforts to create value for our business, I tend to stay client-focused and while I seek to create influence, it is usually to serve our client base by solving a new problem or solving a problem in a new way. Joan is so right in saying that the internal influence is really significant as well. I like to call it "influence" rather than "power" or "authority" because the intent matters. If the EA's intent is to be controlling or manipulative or something that has a negative connotation, it is a power trip and has no place in our businesses.*

I truly believe that most EAs have the Executive's and the organization's best interest in mind, reflecting their actions as pure intent and influential in nature. It is a game of chess, and they are just trying to make sure that the Executive gets to lift their head up from whatever it is they are working on, see the world in the bigger picture, and maybe open the calendar for the person who really needs the Executive's attention.

When my EA knows I have external stakeholders I am trying to spend more time with and I am not able to spend the time that I want, she will go out of her way to make sure that I stay top of mind to them.

An Executive Assistant who is either mistreated, misunderstood, or not well communicated to has the opportunity or ability through their authority (it is granted proxy authority from the Executive) to change the innerworkings of the organization, principally through their influence. EAs can and should impact how that organization receives them and how the Executive receives others. I think that is truly the definition and power of influence.

JOAN: *Talking about internal influence, James, I was thinking about how your EA, Kayla, was influential last year when she went to Universal Engineering's leadership to tell them why sending their assistants to the Office Dynamics' Annual Conference was important and beneficial.*

JAMES: *That's a good example of her internal influence. When my EA brought the ODI Conference to my attention, she did so in a way that was smart and sharp. She saw significant value in our organization supporting attendance in the conference by our leading administrative professionals but knew it was not within the budget for the current fiscal year. She understood what limitations or questions I would foresee, and she said, "Hey, I want to be the champion of this effort, but I believe we need to get additional Executive support from your direct reports in order to have the EAs feel they can go to their strategic partners to request access to this in-person training." I said, "Okay, great! How can I help?" She then said, "I think I should present it to them rather than you. If it is coming from you, it is going to feel a little contrived or it is James telling us how to do things. May I have time with the other Executives, some of whom report to* *you, to present the request and associated expenses?" She prepared a presentation and calendared time with them in an existing meeting, switched up the cadence of the meeting a little bit, and presented the request for budget and support for administrative participation at the ODI conference. There was purely positive feedback, and it did not require political capital from me.*

In hindsight, it was a highly influential moment for my EA. It validated that she was the "real deal" to the other Executives; she took the time; she came prepared; she presented an Executive-quality presentation with ROI, cost-benefit analysis and additional financial and organizational metrics. Quite frankly, the other Executives were not expecting it.

JOAN: *James, thanks for relating a great story about how you value Kayla being an influencer. That was a bold step Kayla took and several assistants in the organization benefited from Kayla's actions.*

JAMES: *There are many kinds of influencers and they come in a variety of their own styles but always are passionate about their style. For example, influencers like those in the social media world take the spotlight and use it to create an action, change an opinion or elicit an emotion. In our business lives, we have similar objectives whether it be to sell a product, demonstrate support for an initiative or showcase key elements of the business' culture.*

In the production world for social media influencers, the people behind the cameras who are crafting the messages and designing the architecture of the interactions are the true influencers. In our business lives, our EA strategic partners are the true influencers, because they are behind the scenes to craft the image and manage the messaging that allows us to be the influencers we want to be.

I have three additional themes to point out about influence.

First, there is the hidden gem in all of this. I remember a specific moment shortly after we hired my current EA, Kayla, to support our company's increasing growth. I remember she said something along the lines of "I don't want recognition; I don't want that attention. That is not what drives me." It was in that moment that I stepped back and knew she was a behind-the-scenes kind of influencer who could actively partner with me to lay the groundwork and architecture needed for our messaging. This style of influence is far-reaching and full of depth. There is something very special about a person whose ego is fully checked at the door and who is self-driven every day to be a positive force in someone else's life. There is nothing quite like it, and I appreciate Kayla's talent and gifts because her being "who she is" organically provides me a highly powerful Competitive Edge.

The second point I think is important to point out is that not every EA/Executive relationship will work well. The most common mismatch I have seen is when the EA needs the spotlight and tries to (subconsciously or consciously) compete with the Executive for it. If the EA needs that constant attention, needs to be thanked regularly and praised publicly, alongside an outward-facing Executive, then the Executive may find themselves unsupported and having to regularly redirect and manage the EA's attempt to seize influence.

A third point about influence is that there could be advantages for an Executive to leverage a spotlight-needy EA by putting them to good use in certain situations. For example, if the Executive's tendencies are more introverted and analytical, it is possible that having an EA who shines in the front would be beneficial. If the intent is pure, the EA can manage the relationships and spotlight in a way that gives the Executive their time and energy back! I think the critical aim is to have an Executive/Executive Assistant matchup that is consistent with allowing each person to do what they were born to do. It is important to ensure synchronization between the EA and Executive; each might be great individually, but it is possible that they aren't great paired together if their individual styles of influence do not complement each other.

JOAN: *There are some innate traits and qualities an individual possesses but they need training to take those to the next level. On the flip side, however, I have recognized through experience that a person might never be able to go deep into a particular skill or attribute. For example, a person who strongly accesses big-picture or abstract thinking will not dramatically switch to being a detailed thinker. It is not in their DNA. I have worked with EAs who are extremely detailed, and they cannot handle abstract thinking, or they need their Executive to spell everything out because they cannot naturally connect the dots.*

JAMES: *It is important to recognize when it is not working out between an EA and Executive. It could be a mismatch in personalities, but often, it is just miscommunication or a lack of communication altogether. Usually, a communication issue can be fixed. You can learn to communicate better with each other over time, but you must be very intentional and candid with each other and say, "Hey, we are not communicating well. What can we do as a partnership to improve?" In a case of a mismatch, it is not personal, but it is personal. You cannot change who you are and who you have been since you were 12 years old. You can fake it for a little while but when your "faking-it-battery" runs out, it will resurface and cause issues. In those situations, it is important to look at the relationship and recognize it is not going to work because of who you are innately. In that scenario,* *focus on kindness, open communication, and understanding, which will lead the Executive and EA through the separation.*

JOAN: *Other factors come into play to help develop a strategic partnership sooner, such as similar values, chemistry, and work styles. Having similar tastes will also speed the formation or deepening of a partnership. This can even be something as small as style of stationery. For example, I do not like a cutesy look in my workplace communications—whether that is an email, personal work stationery, training certificates for participants, conference decorations or the look of printed materials. If my EA understands this, and does not fight my style, it is fantastic! I can trust them to select our company Christmas cards and my personal note cards. When we send gifts to our VIP clients, my EA can make the selection and then run it by me. My EA frequently "nails it" the first time!*

JAMES: *I agree. My style is unique, and I want my Executive Assistant to mirror that style. I am more industrial and minimalist. I do not want that style to be diluted. It has grown to be part of my personal brand. I see Joan in a certain light as well and feel like it is part of her own personal brand! I would say she is classy, professional, and sophisticated, and that is how she "goes to market." We each have EAs that protect and emulate our brands, at least outwardly, so as to reinforce the brand equity of each.*

The Calm in the Storm

Executives work in a chaotic realm. There are a hundred things going on, balls in the air, complexity, crises occur, and last-minute demands. If you have the right assistant as your partner, your assistant will be the calm in the storm. As the leader, you have to show that you are calm in spite of the chaos or what is going on in your life. We are not saying you will not lose your cool in front of your direct reports. But overall, your staff, clients, and stakeholders expect you to look like you are in control.

Your EA is your representative. They are the ones who can calmly manage people, discussions, and emails while you are dealing with the storm. Stellar EAs will be cool and levelheaded. They are grace under fire. They are exemplary ambassadors.

Every day looks incredibly different for assistants. But one thing that is generally true for all assistants: At its core, the role is relationship-based. There is a reason assistants have such high emotional intelligence scores. They have to understand their executives' needs, wants, pet peeves and, most importantly, priorities. They need to not only build a close relationship with their boss, but build relationships with everyone their boss interacts with, and understand those people deeply.

—**Julia Leibowitz**, CEO, Cabinet

Soften the Blow

JAMES: *You cannot always say "Yes" to clients. You cannot show favoritism. As Executives who are time compressed, we usually want to tell it as it is! We do not have time to fluff our words. But your Executive Assistant does. An EA who has excellent communication* *skills and thinks before they speak/write, will massage your message.*

A great EA will spend more time with clients or team members who need extra attention. They will add clarity to your words if context or clarity is lost. They will follow up with recipients to measure and report back on impact, particularly when the messages intended to elicit a specific response or impact. A great EA will apologize on behalf of the Executive IF and ONLY IF it helps to enhance the value of the relationship or move the ball forward for the Executive. A great EA will also shut down any miscommunication or message-spinning. The game of telephone can get ugly once messages leave the Executive's desk, so a great EA can track along with the message to ensure its purity as it is received.

And what does this do for your reputation? WOW!!! A lot.

It is important for the Executive Assistant to have the skill set that will allow them to soften the blow or massage a message. As an engineer, I am very black and white. I tend to be more so than the rest of the world. We design and build structures that either stand firm with a strong foundation OR ELSE they fall over, and people die. That is the world I live in. There is no room for a gray area or flowery messages.

However, when I apply the same seriousness to interpersonal relationships, I have been told that I can be intense or intimidating. For some, I know I tend to be a bit too bold in my language. Sometimes that hurts people's feelings. I have found that by using my EA as a conduit for some messages, I can protect my image and more importantly, work more closely with others to accomplish our shared goals. I can give Kayla the bulleted black and white script, not softened up at all, and she can make it a message for others. She can take a step back, evaluate the intent of the message, and if needed, soften it if the person is particularly sensitive to my messages. Alternatively, if the individual can handle (or needs) the direct communication, she'll pass it through accordingly.

JOAN: *This skill in an EA is high value. One of Melia's greatest strengths is connecting with people. She will take all kinds of time when talking with someone on the telephone whether an EA, Executive, or HR professional. She will answer all their questions and more importantly, connect with them on some personal level. Although I love people and consider myself a "people person" most often when I am communicating in the workplace, I am straight forward and to the point. I am also a more logic-oriented thinker … so sometimes that can come across a little harsh. Often, I am time compressed. I also love to communicate in bullet points. I can tell Melia, "Here is what I want to say. Now you soften it, so the message comes across better."*

JAMES: *It took me a long time to recognize the value in allowing the EA to be this person, the buffer. It started to become more apparent to me as I learned more about how others perceived me. An example that was really impactful for me was when one Executive who reported to me told me that their EA regularly broke down crying after meeting with me. I always viewed my conversation with this EA as a very professional interaction that was focused on a task. We would talk through it. I would give direction, and/or gather input, and then provide direction when requested. Then I would exit the conversation and move along. I found out that this EA needed to be "warmed up" to a conversation by something like, "How was your weekend?" or, "How is your day going?" I learned that our interactions were the least favorite part of that person's job. By team-tagging my EA into that interaction in lieu of me, we improved the EA's life dramatically and removed me from an interaction that was not resulting in what I desired.*

As a very busy Executive, that's hard to do with everybody. I cannot necessarily have a relationship with every single person. But my EA can maintain and manage that relationship moving forward, benefiting us, and ensuring success on the objective. By adding my EA into the mix, I gained another Competitive Edge: a well-executed task and a happier team member. Win-Win!

Well-Connected

Executive Assistants are well-connected internally and externally. And with social media, LinkedIn, Instagram, and Facebook groups, EAs often build massive networks. They can quickly post, "My Executive is traveling to New York City. Can you recommend a fabulous car service?" Within a very short time, your EA will have several recommendations. Voilà!

JOAN: *Insightful and discerning Executive Assistants purposely work to build networks and maintain great relationships. In my opinion as an Assistant and in my teachings, my philosophy for EAs is that they should learn to connect with everyone. They should build relationships with everyone they meet because they never know when and how that person might help in the future. This is also my philosophy as a business owner and CEO. I cannot do life without others. I cannot be successful without others. Even if that person cannot help you, they have a network. Executive Assistants know who to reach out to for:*

- *IT issues.*
- *Great event planning ideas.*
- *Which are the best hotels in a city.*
- *What town car service is most reliable.*
- *Getting the Public Relations firm to write a last-minute press release.*
- *Legal advice.*
- *Past due receivables or payables.*

- *To get that special table at your favorite restaurant.*
- *The best florist.*

And the list goes on. Hopefully, you can see the value in having an EA who is well connected.

An Extension of You

JAMES: *Authority is an interesting topic because once we are put in position of Executives, it is assumed we have earned it or otherwise deserve the role and responsibility. Oftentimes, we have been given it whether we earned it or not. This authority generally is accompanied with responsibility and autonomy, to varying degrees. When we trust our Executive Assistant and the EA trusts the Executive, we can choose to delegate authority and responsibility to the EA and in that authority comes some sense of autonomy. That autonomy means being able to make decisions without having to ask permission or ask for additional acceptance of that decision, however, it is not pure autonomy since the act is an extension of the Executive. When we as Executives give authority and yet we retain the autonomy entirely, the piece of the puzzle that is missing—that is harder to delegate—is the responsibility, and without a sense of autonomy, an EA may struggle to embrace and accept the responsibility.*

You do not lose the responsibility when you delegate authority in autonomy. I think a lot of Executives are hesitant to delegate because they recognize they are still responsible. Let me put it this way:

Authority + Autonomy = Responsibility

Initially, trust is a big thing. If you are new to the strategic partnership relationship with your EA, trust is the most important component of that relationship and as that develops, you will get better at it. As I have experienced having an EA for an extended timeframe, I have learned to be more clear with my directions. I have learned to explain why we are doing something to make sure we are aligned on the vision of where we are headed on a particular task.

Relieve Executive's Decision Fatigue

JOAN: *I first saw the words "decision fatigue" when I read an excellent book called the Founder & the Force Multiplier: How Entrepreneurs and Executive Assistants Achieve More Together by Adam Hergenrother and Hallie Warner.*

As an Executive, I completely relate to decision fatigue. Some days, by the end of the day, I do not want to make One. More. Decision. Or if I am in a rush or am impatient, I may make a decision that I would not normally have made, given more time. There are instances where even the smallest decision looms overwhelmingly large. This is huge reason to have an EA strategic partnership. If you are wondering what types of decisions Executive Assistants make, below is a list of examples provided to me by several Executive Assistants and Administrative Assistants who have attended ODI trainings:

- *Hiring process/on-boarding/interviewer*
- *Training/recommendations/implementation*
- *Leadership meetings/scheduling agenda*
- *Goals & plans/planning/key performance indicator (KPI) measurement*
- *Future planning & construction/project management*
- *Productivity management/down time management*
- *Office tour schedule*
- *Visitor and client luncheons*

- *Cancellations or postponements for meetings, events, or travel*
- *Appreciation outings/logistics/date/venue*
- *Corporate responsibility/community day*
- *Investment*
- *Organizational structure*
- *Day-to day-operations/processes*
- *Emails - scheduling, time off*
- *Research*
- *Procurement*
- *Approval for ordering*
- *Incentives*
- *Intern/mentoring*
- *Availability of technology tools and resources*
- *Managing - routing/timing/prioritizing*
- *Selecting and ordering sympathy flowers, client gifts, holiday cards*
- *Task delegation*
- *Team recognition*
- *Budget*
- *Outsourcing – researching, consulting, reallocations*
- *Tracking progress and managing follow up on any "moving parts" and "wheels in motion" activities*

And people say, "Anyone can be an Executive Assistant and/or an Administrative Assistant. "I do not think so!"

Point Out You r Blind Spots

nces,
ng in the
ur body lan-

?m—blind spots. We talk about this often in
nt or with 360o assessments. Blind spots are
(to us) areas in us we are not able to see but
hen discussing the particular training needs

for a company's Executive Assistants, a Human Resources business partner will tell me what their EAs are missing—what they could do better—or where they need to grow. They can see areas to shore up, to evolve, and to grow that the EAs cannot see. When I work with an Executive to coach their Executive Assistant, the Executive will provide their perspective on their EA's performance, what their EA isn't managing or handling as well as they could, or specific skill sets the Executive wants them to further develop. I have a detailed competency assessment tool I have the Executive complete regarding their EA before I begin the coaching. Many times, the EA thinks they are doing a really good job in a particular area, but the Executive has not ranked them as high on the assessment. We also have the EA rate their Executive on how well they perform in certain areas. I use these tools to help them both grow their "gap" areas or blind spots.

I imagine you are familiar with the Johari Window. Created in 1955 by Joseph Luft and Harry Ingham, the model is used to help individuals better understand themselves and how they are perceived by others.

	Known to Self	Not Known to Self
Known to Others	Open	Blind Spot
Not Known to Others	Hidden	Unkown

When you work closely with your EA, day after day, week after week they get to know you very well. They know your moods, prefer hot spots, weak areas, and strengths. If you are both worki office on the same days, your EA will get to know yo guage; they will know by your walk what kind of mood you are in; they will see your energy and excitement (or lack of). This is great news! Because they can point out your blind spots. As Executives, we are so engrossed in what is going on, how we feel, or preparing mentally for the next big thing, we don't even realize what we might be communicating to our staff, colleagues, or to the world. You need someone who works closely with you, intimately understands you as a person, and has the courage to point out your blind spots. No one else is going to do that for you except your EA, especially if you have built a strategic partnership with that person.

A Wake-Up Call

JOAN: *I was having a challenging week. Projects were not moving forward. I was frustrated that on-site training was not yet being brought back into companies. That Thursday was a rough day for me personally and professionally. On Friday morning, I went to the office as usual. My strategic partner, Melia, walked into my office to discuss something. She said, "I hate to say this, but you look tired this morning. Are you okay? I know it has been a hectic week and yesterday was a rough day for you." By her acknowledgement of my week and by asking if I was okay, Melia:*

- *Showed me she was in tune to me; that she knows me really well.*

- *Gave me permission to express my frustrations, which was a big stress release.*

- *Forced me to pause, get outside of my own irritable head, and made me realize, "Joan, get your act together!" I took a deep breath, mentally and emotionally, regrouped, and moved on.*

Just Because You Can, Does Not Mean You Should

JOAN: *There are many independent, tech-knowledgeable Executives who are so proud they manage everything themselves, such as handling their emails, calendaring, organize paperwork, travel plans, and more. I tell those Executives, "Just because you can do it, it does not mean you should do it. That is not why you are paid the big bucks! Are those activities really the best use of your time?"*

Let me put this into dollars. Let us say a top Executive or high-value director makes $300/hour. If that Executive spends 10 hours weekly dealing with the minutia, in one year they have aggregated 520 hours spent on support work. Here is the salary calculation, which has a poor ROI:

$$520 \text{ hours} \times \$300 = \$156,000$$

Does your organization pay you $156,000 to work on things that do not directly impact the bottom line or grow the business? Were you hired or put into a high-value position to manage emails, schedule your appointments, and book your flights? I do not think so.

You or your company could hire a competent EA for $60,000+ and they will do a darn better job than you!

JAMES: *As an Executive, my job is to hire people to support me, our team, and our clients, which in turn allows me to work at the top of my license. The takeaway is that just because an Executive can do something, it does not mean they should. And if an Executive does not delegate or turn responsibilities over to an EA, neither the Executive nor EA will grow.*

You will have to invest time. The first or second time you ask an EA to perform a task or be responsible for a duty, it will take some time to communicate expectations and parameters, but then that EA will take over that project or task and save you time in long run.

Here is an example from my work: I was responsible to assemble data and prepare a Board presentation every month. It took an inordinate amount of time. I talked to my EA, Kayla, about taking on the project and she enthusiastically agreed. So, for the first two months, I taught her all the ins and outs of how I liked the presentation to be crafted and what data needed to be reported on, and who and provided where the various necessary data came from. I told her I was available for questions to ensure she was prepared, equipped and confident. Kayla took on the task and prepared the Board presentation for the next 10 months ... without involvement from me. That was a great way to gain a Competitive Edge to carve out important blocks of time for me by providing a growth opportunity for my EA and showing her how to be successful doing it.

I think not hiring an EA is sometimes a cop-out for someone who is not a strong delegator. Yes, sometimes the business cannot support the additional payroll, but that is not the case as often as companies or business owners use that excuse for not hiring an EA.

"Not having an assistant doesn't make you an
enlightened leader. It makes you a handicapped leader.
The truth is you can't do it all yourself."

—Jan Jones, Author of The CEO's Secret Weapon

JAMES: *When Joan and I were regularly attending our Las Vegas-based CEO peer group, we learned about the acronym "HERD." Often when our peer CEOs were issue processing, they asked the CEO with the issue to identify:*

- *Hours. How many hours is this problem or issue or challenge creating for you? Or how many hours are you spending on "X" that your EA or someone else could be handling?*

- *Emotion. What are your emotions around the situation? Emotions take up time, space, and energy.*

- *Relationships. How is this issue affecting your work and personal relationships? Is it stressing you out and making it difficult to be "present"?*

- *Dollars. How does this issue affect your bottom line? And is the amount of energy and angst around processing this issue and trying to develop a solution costing you (or your company) time and energy that could be better spent working on your deliverables as an Executive?*

In the earlier scenario, it is not just about your salary of $156,000. How many hours did it take you to get through emails, schedule and reschedule your appointments or research flight schedules? How many hours did you spend thinking about these issues? What did you **not do** that **only you** could be doing instead? Not to rub salt into the wound, but while you were handling the minutia, you were not:

- Servicing a client.
- Chasing a project.
- Working one-on-one with your team.
- Creating lasting relationships internally or externally.
- Solving a thorny issue that only you can handle.
- Vision casting for the next season or company objective.
- Sharpening and enhancing your knowledge and subject matter expertise.
- Learning new skills to propel your career forward.

This is not to say that calendaring is a small, unmeaningful task. Complex calendaring takes discernment, diplomacy, and competency.

There are people who love to support other people and are darn good at it—highly trained, highly effective, and simply **just better** than you are at doing those things. Why not put a remarkable, talented, and skilled EA on the team? It will give you a Competitive Edge.

It is mind-blowing to me that, using Joan's sports analogy, if you have somebody who is a great running back, why not hire them and let them be the running back? If you have an EA who is uniquely qualified and extremely passionate about it, you are going to get every dollar and more out of that value 100% every time. And the other part is you get to do what you **really** love! What Executive would not want that?

Like most Executives or business owners, we too want to perform work that feeds our soul; plays to our strengths. Partnering with a great EA strategic partner will free us to do more of the things we love, that could very well *impact our community, business, industry, and the world. A great EA will take ownership of it (whatever "it" is) and they will say, "Show me that, give me that, I'm going to take it over."*

JOAN: *As a previous long-time EA and speaking for today's Executive Assistants, let me tell you **we love what we do**. It is our Career of Choice, and we are proud of it. First and foremost, we love partnering with our Executives and helping them shine bright. Executive Assistants want to:*

- *Make our Executives' lives easier—take away the stress, put out the fires, and work magic that will delight.*
- *Be the go-to person and continue to develop areas of expertise.*
- *Improve work quality and processes.*
- *Be Siri, Google, and Alexa rolled into one.*
- *Seamlessly deliver work.*
- *Employ our attitude of service.*
- *Help Executives achieve their goals and the company mission.*
- *Deliver exemplary service on every task and project.*
- *Provide our Executive a Competitive Edge.*
- *Gather research for a speech.*
- *Prepare stats/charts.*
- *Design a complex PowerPoint presentation.*
- *Assemble cost history for the fiscal budget.*

What do we want? We want to be:

- *Recognized for our hard work.*
- *Valued, appreciated, and acknowledged.*
- *Part of the succession plan.*
- *Compensated for the value we bring to our Executives and companies.*
- *Included in staff meetings, department head meetings, and Executive retreats.*
- *Supported in our professional development.*
- *Strategic business partners with our Executive.*

In summary, an EA can be an Executives' strategic business partner, company confidante, analytical person and "got your back" huckleberry, working to help you achieve company initiatives. You, as the Executive, need to set the tone for the partnership, engage your EA with meaningful tasks, and above all, RELEASE them to work their magic. Then stand back and be amazed.

A Word About Personal Assistants

An EA can be a Personal Assistant (PA) too. Or an EA can be only an EA. This is something that you, as the Executive, need to think about before you hire for this position. Additionally, you should also consider if the company allows EAs to perform tasks of a personal nature and whether a company policy prohibits staff from driving their personal cars (accident liability) in pursuit of company business.

For James, the preferred role for his support is primarily EA but sometimes he has tasks that are personal in nature that his EA will offer to help with. Once in a while, James will ask for assistance on personal tasks if his work tasks require his undivided attention and the task is not overly intimate or personal (an example is booking travel for a family vacation).

JAMES: *My EA knows my travel preferences, as well as those of my family. She is the best person to manage travel plans IF my spouse is unable or unwilling to do it. Oftentimes, I'll want to surprise my spouse with a trip or special event, and thus, my EA will be instrumental in the planning of this personal event.*

The key to the EA/PA scope of duties is you must have the discussion about expectations upfront when you are interviewing for a new EA or if the organization assigns an EA to you. That said, your situation could change over time. Maybe you are married but then you go through a divorce. Or maybe your spouse becomes seriously ill, requiring extensive therapy treatments. In these cases, you will probably want assistance with your calendar and management of personal issues in addition to professional initiatives.

Meet Kerri, Wende, and Melinda: EA/PAs Extraordinaire

JOAN: *I personally know and have worked with these three amazingly talented, multi-dimensional Executive Assistants. They all work for high-profile CEOs. They are basically on call 24/7 to run their Executive's personal and professional life. They execute their work with heart and soul. They feel highly responsible for their Executive's success and shine brightest when called upon to manage a crisis or handle an emergency.*

Of course, not every Executive reading this book will need this type of support. I just want you to know it is possible if and when the time comes for you.

The Challenge of a Virtual Setting

Working "on the field" as a team is a challenge for any organization relying solely on virtual interactions. It can be difficult to feel like a team and to operate "on the field" in a 100% virtual setting because it is easy to miss body language cues, spontaneity, to have on-the-spot problem solving or creative meetups, or to easily assess each other's tone or mood.

It is not impossible to do so, but it requires careful relationship nurturing to achieve the same level of cohesiveness found in day-to-day office interactions. The Executives and EAs who thrive in virtual working relationships have to work hard at it. They are intentional about their partnership, processes, and daily operating functions. They know the importance of regular verbal communication and keeping each other informed as each piece of the puzzle moves into place.

What can you do?

- Leverage the strategies presented in this book.
- Plan to over-communicate.
- Encourage questions when assigning tasks or projects to ensure you share clear objectives and expectations.
- Ask your EA to offer feedback on your teaming strategies – what can you do better?
- Periodically discuss the health of your partnership with your EA.
- Request feedback about what you should start doing and stop doing.
- Ask your EA if they have encountered any roadblocks while pursuing a task or project objectives. If they have, use your authority to help remove the roadblocks to ensure successful completion.
- Be flexible – recognize it may not be possible to solely work 100% virtual or 100% in the office.
- If you must reach out to your EA after hours or on holidays or weekends, be respectful of your EAs personal schedule.
- Clearly state when an assigned task is of a personal nature, such as booking a family vacation, and ensure the EA has everything required (such as your personal credit card information, legal names of all travelers, frequent flyer numbers and TSA preCheck information) to successfully complete the personal task.

Addressing the "Elephant in the Room"
(Having a Personal Relationship Without Getting Personal)

JAMES: *This may be a touchy topic for some, and I am taking particular care to craft the message effectively, concisely, and without bias, but the fact of the matter is that there are few relationships in our lives as CEOs that are as personal as that of the strategic partnership with our EA. With regard to this statement, gender and sexual orientation are irrelevant; to be effective, the relationship has to be tight. This type of close work relationship may evoke in some a varying degree of concern regarding the "single cell" partition between one's personal life and work life. Where should we place the line between the two? Joan and I debated for many hours about how to appropriately discuss this topic, and frankly, Joan was hesitant to even include it. From my perspective though, I was insistent that we address it as the "elephant in the room" because we have the legacy issue of those who came before us.*

The business culture that has been portrayed by Hollywood to the masses cannot be mistaken for the real world. Although "Madmen" and "9 to 5" might make for good (?) entertainment, they do not reflect reality.

Executives cannot be fearful of having powerful and meaningful relationships with their EAs simply because they are fearful of potential misperception. Joan and I believe it is crucial to address anything which might prevent an Executive from the consideration of hiring an EA or which might inhibit the Executive and EA professional relationship from developing.

Mission Critical Challenge
(How To Have a Personal Relationship Without Getting Personal)

Your life is not "The Wolf of Wall Street" or an episode from HBO's "Mad Men." The Office Manager is not walking around the office feeding the Executive Assistants birth control pills and filling up the scotch decanters for the Executives. You WILL lose EVERYTHING if you cross ethical or moral boundaries in any inappropriate fashion. This goes for all parties involved, because there is not a single form of risk for one side of this issue.

That said, this CANNOT deter you from building a strong, personal relationship with your Executive Assistant. Frankly, the opposite should be true; with a powerful relationship, you and your EA can battle any rumors, change management, and unexpected situations by SHOWING the right way to work together to fulfill the corporate initiatives you are responsible to achieve. Lead from the front. Show the team what it means to be agnostic and accepting of diversity, equity, inclusiveness and belonging within your business and in your life. Show that gender and sexual orientation has nothing to do with business relationships in the modern business world through your actions, through your words, and through your kindness.

Go to lunch with your EA. Meet for coffee outside the office. Ask how their family is doing, how their vacation was, and offer support when their loved ones face health challenges. Build trust in the relationship over time and as your business relationship grows, be cognizant of the perception of others. Always maintain mutual respect, professionalism, and (surprised that I write it again?) offer kindness toward one another.

SUMMARY
PART 1

James

A Tale of Two Executives: One With an EA and One Without

While other Executives are using their own voice in their heads as their sounding board, you are using your Executive Assistant as a sounding board.

While others are sorting through their thoughts on their own and thinking about various strategic initiatives in a solo fashion with its inherent blind spots, you are organizing your thoughts and strategic initiatives through your Executive Assistant.

While the Executive who does not have a Competitive Edge is trying to manage the 20 most important relationships they have, you as an Executive with an Executive Assistant can effectively impact exponentially more relationships through your Executive Assistant.

How Is This Possible?

While an Executive without an EA will work on five things one by one each day, the Executive with a Competitive Edge will work on three high-quality decisions or initiatives daily with an EA working on 25 things concurrently.

While an Executive is managing their calendar and booking appointments, an EA can push the Executive to focus on professional initiatives and needle-moving interactions, all while ensuring they are where they need to be, at the time they need to be there, pre-read done, prepared, and ready to act.

While an Executive is creating a vision in their own words, an Executive and EA team can create a vision that is actionable, executable, laser-sharp, and messaged in words that everyone can understand and drive forward to achieve. By leveraging work through an EA, this can be done with surgical precision!

These are just a few of the critical elements to gaining a Competitive Edge.

Traits Needed in the Executive Role

I aim to lead with empathy and maintain a commitment to kindness in both external and internal relationships. If there is only one trait that I can align my team around, it would be kindness every single time. The world can be cruel but through a stewardship guided by kindness, our organization can ensure positive energy, and momentum through our most valuable asset, our people. There is so much chaos, pent-up negative emotion, and misplaced negative energy that if I can just boil it down to kindness, compassion, and a sense of understanding, in my experience I have found our team members, partners, and clients can support each other through any hardship. Kindness, as demonstrated by an Executive and Executive Assistant team, is the most important Competitive Edge.

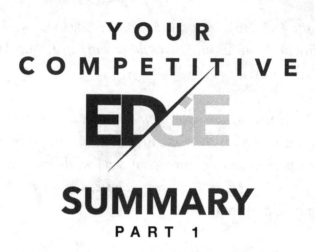

YOUR COMPETITIVE EDGE

SUMMARY
PART 1

Joan

The Executive With an EA

Put simply, while other Executives are:
- *Answering non-important emails.*
- *Booking their own meetings, catering, and conference room reservations ... and then modifying them five times[3].*
- *Booking and managing their own travel, including last-minute flight cancellations.*
- *Monitoring follow-up items, even those that are minutia.*
- *Filtering the "noise."*
- *Trying to maintain a "pulse" on their team.*

You are:
- *Working on mission-critical assignments.*
- *Building strong relations with top-tier clients.*

---

[3] *If you think using a calendar app to 'plop' meetings into an empty space on an empty date is the answer, you really don't understand the importance of strategically mapping appointments, meetings, and travel. No app, no matter how techie or modern, can replace the holistic thinking of a savvy Executive Assistant!*

- *Closing deals.*
- *Attending industry events, wining, dining, and networking.*
- *Doing more of what you love.*
- *Creating and communicating the vision for your organization in an effective, powerful way.*
- *Taking more time to lead with empathy, kindness, and clarity.*
- *Coaching and mentoring your key people.*
- *Partnering with Board members.*
- *Expanding your sphere of influence.*
- *Interpreting new information on the fly so you can plan for multiple scenarios.*
- *Enjoying time with your family.*
- *Managing your health and keeping stress at bay.*

What Executive would not want an EA strategic partner?

Joan's Caveat:
CAUTION There Is No Magic

At this point, you are likely feeling excited and (hopefully) ready to jump in with both feet. That is great! But before you do, a quick warning and disclaimer: This book is not magic. Simply reading it will not create the outcomes you are seeking. It only works IF you work it. You need to implement what you learn. You and your EA must be willing participants who will work together to form a partnership. I am confident that the methods outlined in this book will work for you, but we accept no responsibility for non-action. Without your commitment to leverage what you have read; this book will simply be just words on paper.

To assist you in the implementation process, I recommend the following:
- *Give every process improvement at least three weeks before determining whether to keep or discard it. Research shows that it takes at least 21 days to make or break a habit. Do not try something for three days and give up when it feels uncomfortable. Give it time.*
- *Track your progress along the way. Monitor what is working and what is not. Be flexible to modify or change it up so that it has a custom fit for you and your EA.*
- *Keep the dialogue open with your Executive Assistant as you take this journey together. It is a critical part of the process and cannot be overemphasized.*

GEMS TO LEAD BY

PART 1

- Operate with kindness, first and always.
- As the Executive, whether we delegate authority and autonomy to our EA, the responsibility still sits with us.
- In a case of a mismatch, it is not personal ... but it is personal. You cannot change who you are and who you have been since you were 12 years old. You can fake it for a little while but when your "faking-it-battery" runs out, it will resurface and cause issues.
- With an Executive Assistant who grows into a Strategic Partner, you can **exponentially** increase impact.
- The EA role is so much bigger than what most people perceive.
- EAs might be "behind the scenes," but their presence makes a difference. They can create a powerful ripple effect through the organization.
- A great EA will watch your back and look down the rails for oncoming trains like no one else in the organization will do for you.
- Who is your sounding board? Who, at work, will listen to you rant and rave without judgment? Who will soften your message? Or be your day-to-day spokesperson? Your EA.
- Delegate, get your EA in the business, tell your EA why you make the decisions you make so when they face a similar situation, they

know how you would approach it, or they know who to go to for sound advice.

- Most EAs have the Executive's and the organization's best interest in mind, reflecting their actions as pure intent and influential in nature.

- You, as the Executive, need to set the tone for the partnership, engage your EA with meaningful tasks, and above all, RELEASE them to work their magic. Then stand back and be amazed.

TECTONIC
SHIFTS

A VERY PERSONAL STORY

JOAN: *Never in my lifetime did I consider a pandemic would happen—especially in the good old USA! When we first heard about the pandemic, many of us thought, "In a few weeks, we will be back to our old lives. We will return to our offices; cruising and air travel will resume. We will go along our merry way." I am not going to review 2020 – 2022 as I am tired of listening to that broken record. We all know what transpired.*

Instead, I want to focus on the aftermath. But before I do that, I want to share a very personal story.

I experienced three major crises between 2008 – 2015:

- *In 2008, my husband was diagnosed with pancreatic cancer (at age 57) and passed away at 60. It was a very intense battle. While you might be thinking my husband was the sick one, I had my own frightful experiences, too. I was his full-time caregiver while running a business, taking care of the household, and watching a man I dearly loved wither away little by little. Then came that awful first year of being a widow after 34 years of marriage.*

- *On July 4, 2014, my neighbor drove me to the local emergency room where I was later diagnosed with a very rare massive brain tumor called a clival chordoma. And, unbeknownst to me, at the same time, I had contracted bacterial meningitis. I was deathly ill. I was transported to St. John's Hospital in Santa Monica, California, where I underwent a 13-hour brain sur-*

gery to remove 95% of the tumor. Post operation, I experienced ICU psychosis for two days—it was horrific and very scary. Two weeks later, while recovering at a family member's house in Los Angeles, I had a grand mal seizure and was rushed back to the hospital. (I am happy to report that following four months of recovery, I was leading a full happy life again.)

- *One year later, in 2015, I had open heart surgery. The bacterial meningitis had seeded on my mitral valve. The original heart surgery went very well. One week later when I went for my follow-up visit, the doctors discovered fluid around my heart which had to be drained. I was not allowed to leave the hospital. I was whisked away to prepare for drainage of the fluid. Unfortunately, the physician working to drain the fluid from around my heart instead punctured my heart. I was immediately put back in surgery and then remained in the hospital another week. I am a fighter and eventually healed from all of that.*

These were three very good reasons why I was so thankful to have a strategic EA who kept the business running while I was tending to my personal life.

What I know for sure is that when a crisis strikes, we just get through it. We manage it. We do it. What I also know is that post-traumatic stress is real. It is after the dust settles, realization sets in, and we think, "Oh, my gosh! What the heck happened?"

That is kind of where I am right now as I reflect on the past two years. "Oh, my gosh! What happened to our workplaces, to the things we were so familiar with; the way we worked; and people wanting to be together in the same room?" I also wonder about what happened to many EAs I knew whose companies felt they were no longer necessary. I realize that because of the pandemic, there were some amazing innovations. We all learned we could work from home and be productive. My team and I were able to pivot all our onsite training to live, virtual training. We converted our in-person conference to be fully virtual in 2020; in 2021, we hosted our conference both in-person and live-streamed. We became very good at pivoting and reinventing how we operated. We had to.

JAMES: *Our organization's COVID experience was very unique. The pandemic ramped up while we were in due diligence for recapitalization of our primary engineering company into a new private equity-backed firm. We were not eligible for federal or state grants or loans due to the complexity of the financial requirements of the deal. Nor could we afford to lose anyone. With our services needed to support construction, development, and life-safety inspections, we were busier than ever.*

However, it was much more difficult to accomplish the same tasks. How do you leave a signed, hard copy of your report on the project site if there is no access to a site superintendent? How do you review the plans and permits (hard copy) if you are not allowed to be near other team members? How do you collaborate to resolve as-built issues with welded connections if the structural engineer cannot travel from one city to another to visit the site? These, and many other issues, arose early in the pandemic and our business had to pivot. While virtual inspections were allowed by code and Operating Procedures for most government agencies, very few jurisdictions allowed for these tools pre-pandemic. Suddenly, virtual inspections (FaceTime, Zoom, GoToMeeting, etc.) were all normal video tools used to supplement site visits. Jurisdictions were limited by their organized labor affiliations and other labor constraints, while as a private business, we were told to "figure it out." Fortunately, we were prepared to pivot; we announced that our staff should "work from the safest location, outside!" Our office staff pushed to remote work, but instead of working from home, most worked from job sites and tailgates. Our pre-COVID focus on IT connectivity, tablets, laptops, VPNs, etc. had really paid off; with some serious focus and quick movement, our IT team had our entire organization mobile enough to work from wherever, whenever. We were able to maintain utilization (hours billed to our clients for services provided) and able to manage the rest of the due diligence process, closing process, and even the integration process.

For us, the tsunami we faced was the fact that we COULDN'T stop or slow down. My partner, Joe, (Chief of Staff) would keep me updated on California, Nevada, and local government rulings daily. We managed communicating to our team regularly. While we shouldered the risks of staying open, we balanced them with the risks of closing the doors. I traveled regularly for work and quarantined numerous times due to exposure. During one "close call" I quarantined between my truck parked in the office parking lot (so I could easily access our server from within the firewalls, a loophole that has since been closed) and the pool house at my residence to not expose the family to any illnesses I had picked up during my travels. Although I was not afraid for my own well-being, I certainly did not want to potentially hurt anyone else by spreading the bug. On one such day, while working from my truck in the parking lot, Joe asked me via text, "Why are you smiling? You are working from your truck; I am inside the lobby, and I can see your grin from here!" I responded, "Joe, do you not get it? I have a renewed sense of purpose. THIS is what I am here for. THIS is what I have been waiting for. THIS TEAM, their well-being, and their ability to feed their families, is what I have been preparing for. I am not afraid. I am invigorated by this challenge and ready to own it. Not only will we survive this, but we will THRIVE through it." He laughed and said, via text, "You are insane." Maybe.

But I was not in solitary confinement, even when quarantined. I had the Chief of Staff, and equally important, my EA, ready to go to battle with me. Without them, I am not certain that our organization would have grown 200% in revenue and headcount in 2 years (much of which was done by additional acquisitions during the pandemic). Without them, I am not certain that I would not have REALLY gone insane ... they helped keep me grounded, focused, and determined with a sense of purpose.

As of this writing (summer, 2022) it seems we have all made it through the tsunami. Now let us look at what has transpired.

The Hybrid Workplace

JOAN: *Numerous studies and research point to the many benefits of a hybrid workplace. (Steelcase 360 has several published studies.)*

Employees:
- *Love working from home.*
- *Do not have to worry about their workplace wardrobe when WFH.*
- *Save money on clothes and gas.*
- *Save time not driving to work.*
- *Have more time with their families.*
- *Flexible schedules.*
- *Remote work can level the playing field for marginalized groups, removing barriers to entry for many people.*
- *Better work/life balance.*
- *And the list goes on and on ...*

Employers:

- *Save vast sums through reduced site expenses: utilities, cafeteria food and products, janitorial, postage, copying machines and paper, rent, parking and transportation subsidies.*
- *Do not have to deal with workplace conflict in the office.*
- *Have happier employees.*
- *Do not have to enforce certain rules.*
- *Give leaders previously unheard-of opportunities to hire and retain diverse teams.*
- *Eliminate travel costs, hot spot subscriptions, meeting and offsite conference expense.*
- *Increased employee retention.*
- *Fewer meetings scheduled.*

EA Significance

Your EA is significant because there are multiple, complex moving issues you have to deal with around remote work: employees coming into the office on different days; unplanned absences required due to quarantine protocols, illness or hospitalizations; virtual and in-person meetings to schedule and IT issues to manage; hard copies, postal mail, and office supplies to mail to employees at their homes; employees having very specific, urgent, and different needs; observance of safety health protocols; local and regional mandates and restrictions to follow; mental health issues for employees and their loved ones who are struggling with isolation, AND who will help to keep up morale?

The Evolving Role of the Executive

JOAN: *I love to read about workplace changes, trends, and what we can expect. Then I think about how that will affect my clients' worlds, EAs and their Executives, my industry, and myself as a leader. In February 2022, I read an excellent piece on The Evolving Executive by Dana Wilkie. Dana is a writer for SHRM's Executive Network newsletter, EN: Brief (SHRM stands for Society Human Resource Management).*

Without going into details, here is what is required of today's Executive for business to move forward in the new normal:

- *Transparency around the organization*
- *Empathy*
- *Work flexibility*
- *Relinquishing the role of monarch*
- *Collaboration*
- *Hire for connections, social capital, strategic mastery, and agility.*
- *Being a servant leader who operates with vulnerability and authenticity*
- *Being an approachable human*

EA Significance

Your EA can ensure you are staying connected ... even when you cannot be connected because they understand why your connections are so important. Your EA can send messaging, write note cards, or craft an email just to say "hello" to the folks you want or need to keep engaged. A savvy EA can respond on your behalf to LinkedIn messages or Facebook posts. Your EA can observe how you interact with your direct reports or other staff and make sure you are being empathetic when necessary.

The Future-Minded Leader

JOAN: *According to BetterUp Labs 64-page Report/Winter 2022, future-minded leadership is about preparing for multiple possible futures along with the roadblocks and setbacks that may occur along the way. Additionally, the report states, "Managers high in future-minded leadership skills have future-ready teams."*

EA Significance

Your EA is vital because you cannot possibly keep an eye on everything. You do not have the time to read every piece of information that mentions future trends or where your industry, state, region or country is heading. A great EA can research this information for you and provide you with a summary. They can be your ears and eyes on what is on the horizon. They can set up Google alerts for important clients so when news breaks that could impact your business, they can let you know.

A great EA who acts as a Strategic Partner can help you

to anticipate, forecast, and navigate the future. This will give you a Competitive Edge. A great EA is one who has learned to stay informed and to understand the potential ramifications for you and the organization. This EA can also work alongside you to build future-ready teams.

The Need for Speed

JOAN: *I am sure you would agree we are time compressed. We all feel the need for speed. If we are operating full throttle, we also are not taking time to:*

- *Massage our messages or re-read them for tone or word selection.*
- *Think of all the details or the many deadlines looming.*
- *Consider the impact of our actions.*
- *Be empathetic toward an employee.*
- *Communicate the big picture to our team.*
- *Closely look at our calendars to identify conflicts.*
- *Strategically manage the Big Picture and the organization's underlying currents.*

EA Significance

Your EA can be the one to do the items listed above. They can focus on the details, think about the ramifications, show empathy by listening to an employee, communicate the big picture on your behalf. Your EA can also slow you down by holistically giving you breathing space on your calendar or just telling you, "Slow it down." They can also help you manage the Big Picture and advise you about underlying currents. They can help you by reading communications for word selection and tone. They can track and follow up on deadlines.

The World Is Getting Much Smaller

JOAN: *Although the world got much bigger in the world connectedness during the pandemic, it also got much smaller. We lost logistical boundaries. We experienced work and home overlapping 24/7, weekends, holidays, and "vacations" which were spent at home. The work came non-stop. Getting mail to the right person was a nightmare to process. We felt disconnected from our organizations, the "water cooler" conversations, and groups/clubs we belonged to at work. Websites and organization charts were slow to update. We were unaware of personnel departures or hiring. We lost contact with fitness buddies who worked out next to us at the company fitness center!*

Through all of this, the EA was the one who kept the team connected and therefore able to remain in sync.

Thanks to technology, ODI training could and did still happen worldwide, but I still depended on my EA for many details: sending participants the course training guides; coordinating the training *appointments with client participants, HR staff, and managers; creating virtual meeting rooms; facilitating connections and troubleshooting connectivity issues for participants; managing the chat during the training meeting and helping with post-training follow-up. All this vital work meant I could instead focus on writing training materials which were on point for the client, managing cultural knowledge transfer which might be needed in international settings, and ensuring that the materials, exercises, graphics, and charts would be precisely helpful for the intended audience, and so on. Because my EA did her work, it allowed me the bandwidth necessary to check **every** page of **every** module to confirm how a specific page might be interpreted by this audience and industry, and would a particular word have the same nuance and meaning in another culture? I could not have done it without my EA's expertise.*

EA Significance

Your EA is your connector. They are time zone monitors. They have the ability and time to learn about cultural protocol and etiquette, and to ensure you are apprised so you do not embarrass yourself or your company.

The Great Resignation

JOAN: *The great resignation has created a lot of empty holes in organizations across the country and in every industry. Who will be doing that work? Who is picking up the slack?*

EA Significance

A stellar EA can manage multiple projects and tasks. They are open to taking on numerous assignments at one time and are experienced jugglers. And if they cannot handle everything, they will find someone who can. EAs have a spectacularly diverse and wide network of colleagues with specialized knowledge. If the EA does not know, they know someone who does!

Heavily Trimmed Executive Assistant Staff

JOAN: *During the pandemic, many organizations drastically cut their administrative and Executive Assistant staff, leaving Executives to share support staff. This action made it very difficult for the EAs and for the people they are supporting. This affects work productivity and stress tolerance[4]. Stress tolerance is the threshold at which an individual can effectively and consistently deal with and manage stressful situations. Stress is a normal biochemical reaction that occurs when the prefrontal cortex of the brain secretes and regulates a stress hormone called dopamine. A small amount of stress can be beneficial to a person by increasing focus on routine tasks and/or trigger warnings against potential threats. However, elevated levels of stress can impair cognitive function (i.e., concentration), interfere with relationships at home and/or work, and lead to detrimental future health issues.*

---

[4] *The source for definition of stress tolerance, www.workplacetesting.com*

When an organization overloads an Executive Assistant with too many people to support, the EA will suffer and so will the quality of their work. Some EAs simply do not have the human capacity to manage so many projects, tasks, and multiple people.

I am not saying we have to revert to one EA for every Executive. I know that is not going to happen. But some organizations are assigning five or more busy people to one EA. That simply is not fair to the EA who is trying their best to handle everything in a 40-hour or less week. If you have the ability to hire an EA, then you should. It just makes good sense.

EA Significance

Sharing an EA with three (or more) people is difficult unless the other leaders have a light workload. Often you do not get the adequate attention you need, which could impact results. And if any emergencies occur that require the EA's singular attention, it means that until it is resolved, the other Executives have no recourse. They will also need to manage their expectations about whose priorities are to be handled first!

Virtual Meeting Burnout

JOAN: *I have heard complaints that Executives (and other individual contributors) are in more meetings in a day than pre-2020 because they do not have travel time. They can easily go from one virtual* *meeting to the next to the next. While many Executives were already burnt out from in-person meetings and traveling from one meeting to another, they did have lengthier breaks between meetings for "walking through the buildings" or travel time. I see an upside to that, though, as the scenery change provided a mental break. I know when I am driving, I come up with all sorts of ideas for my business. Also, in pre-2020, the proximity to colleagues and subject matter experts was so frequent and easy! As you would walk through the hallways or building, you would run into people. You would talk about a project or just check in with each other. Running into people was, and still is, mentally stimulating.*

EA Significance

EAs will intently review your schedule and purposely make sure you get breaks. They will block time for you to work on an important project. They will not say "Yes" to every meeting or "Yes" when a time is not convenient for you. Hopefully, they are also aware of the new phenomena, camera fatigue and will break up your schedule accordingly. They may even make sure you have lunch out one or two days a week to break up the monotony.

The World Is a Lot Less Personal

JOAN: *Let us admit it. We live in an impersonal world where we frequently see that people do not respect each other like they used to. We read and hear about it daily. We see the toll this is taking on* society. There is a lot of recent chatter about the recently launched metaverse, which represents a highly interactive three-dimensional virtual world where users can trade land, buildings, and other digital assets in the metaverse and explore the space using their personalized avatars. Yes, you can now live and work in a fake world through virtual reality. You can purchase homes in this virtual space and dress your avatar in designer clothes. You can attend meetings and "travel" to distant lands from the comfort of your couch. Talk about escaping reality! This advancement combined with other types of entertainment and means of communicating (social media, texting, emailing instead of phone calls) further distance us from our colleagues, managers, family, and friends. How will we address the impact against our personal and business relationships? In an article published on LinkedIn[5], author Michelle Calloway advised that NOW is the time to nurture your relationships, both personal and professional, by asking yourself:

- What can you do to make sure your friends and loved ones stay close in relationship with you?
- What can you do to make your customers feel valued, seen, heard, and appreciated?

I would further add that your EA can help you maintain appropriate contact and help you decide when "in-person face time" is beneficial to your client, direct reports, and business objectives ... another way you can operate with a Competitive Edge. Leverage your EA to provide direct input about investing time where most needed.

---

[5] Will the Metaverse Affect Human Relationships? - A Tech with Heart Episode with Michelle Calloway, published November 11, 2021.

EA Significance

Your EA will add the personal touch to help you maintain appropriate contact with clients, direct reports, organization, and overall business objectives. For those of you who only want a virtual relationship with your EA, this affects you as well. Processing work that way is okay as long as your EA is giving high-touch concierge service to your customer, clients, stakeholders, and teams. Otherwise, this does not give you the Competitive Edge.

JAMES: *We are in this crazy time trying to roll along in business while grappling with the pandemic, The Great Resignation, hyper-inflation, supply chain strain, etc. With these economic stresses, the employee-employer relationship is at an all time low. We may see an all new era where the employees are in control as more people demand that their employers allow them to work remotely or from home, for at least a portion of the work week. I feel like a lot of the social interaction has started to slip even further. Joan, how much damage do you think this pandemic has done to communication, the interpersonal relationships, and the in-person communication inside of businesses?*

JOAN: *It has created a lot of hardship and not just from my perspective. I am hearing from hundreds of Executive Assistants around the world. Many of them feel isolated and detached from their company. In the beginning, it was fun to work from home and many EAs loved working from home and still do. But they noted they felt some disconnect, a lack of community and camaraderie. They miss the friendships and chats at the coffee café or company lounge.*

Why Is Working in the Office So Beneficial to Business?

JOAN: *When we were working in the office on a regular basis, we frequently experienced spontaneous brainstorming. Suddenly, I would think of a great idea. I would walk out of my office to share my idea with my team. Before you knew it, we would have all sorts of creative conversations that ultimately led to hosting better events, servicing our clients at an even higher level, streamlining a bulky process, increasing revenue, and more.*

A psychologist recently wrote, "As human beings we are not designed to go with this isolation and social distancing for this long [of a] time. We are designed for temporary setback in crisis. We are not designed to go two whole years doing what we've been doing and living this way (2020-2022). We're a human being."

JAMES: *This is a brilliant point. I think we can anchor a bit of our conversation around these communication tools. These tools were created for the gaps when you cannot meet in-person. They are not the solution for the long haul. We are social beings. I thrive on social interaction inside of the business world. It is part of who I am. I want to be around people. Without that interaction, I feel like we are losing a lot of the cultural progress that was made in American business and the modern global business environment. I think we have gone backwards 20 years culturally in business, just because of the shift between "in-person" experiential work and the new "work from home" chant. Let us be real … work from home is not an effective solution for most. I am not saying it cannot be a short-term solution for some or even a long-term solution for a very few, but it should not replace the human interaction and interpersonal growth that the in-person office environment provides.*

We have learned that we can survive and thrive for periods of time because we are resilient. We have to carve our way through the negative impact from it though. Weariness from digital networks, limited downtime due to continuous connection, inadequate unwind time during travel from work to home, and many more elements of the work-home life relationship are completely upside down.

*There are digital tools to survive and thrive for **short** durations to fill those gaps when there is something going on, i.e., the Executive has to travel for a month or step away from the business for a family leave of absence or whatever else. For example, Zoom or Teams can give you a "face-to-face" meeting (although you cannot*

"These tech tools were created for the gaps when you cannot meet in person. They are not the solution for the long haul. We are social beings."

—James Bristow, PhD

read body language like you can in-person). You can use "tasking" apps, like Microsoft To Do, to create lists and manage assignments without having to hold an in-person meeting, but it is difficult to prioritize and pick up on perceived importance between the parties using the tool. We can use these tools to survive and maintain progress, but each tool presents one or more limitations that must be evaluated. We have to be cognizant that, no matter what, the relationship is better in-person, and these apps can never fully replace that.

I believe that some virtual assistants would suggest this may not be the case or Executives who prefer a virtual assistant will suggest that is not the case. Most humans need to interact with other humans and a metaverse simply does not replace the real world, no matter how realistic we try to make it. I do not know that was ever up for debate despite robots and computers trying to suggest otherwise. I am certainly not suggesting that virtual assistants are not valuable or meaningful; alternatively, I am suggesting that whenever possible, an Executive Assistant and the Executive should meet in person to MAXIMIZE VALUE in the relationship.

That said, I would personally not have a solely virtual assistant if an in-person EA is an option. Unless your EA is doing digital communication, calendaring, and trip planning, (the tip of the iceberg), I think it has to be in-person to be a successful relationship. I cannot imagine what my life and career would look like if I only had a virtual assistant because the personal relationship that grows and builds to become a strategic partnership could not happen for me. I am a young Executive. I am connected. I am into technology and not afraid of it, but I cannot imagine what it would be like to lead businesses without a person committed and dedicated to supporting the initiatives, real time and in person with me.

Proof that I do not hate technology: I use the Microsoft To Do app that functionally serves as an agenda for a daily huddle with my EA, and for my regular one-on-one meetings with my other direct reports. I can reorganize and reprioritize within the application with some sense of effectiveness. I can have a task with subtasks to show the sequential steps needed to successfully execute a primary initiative. I often add due dates to clearly outline what I want done and more importantly, when it needs to be done by. I use it as a collaboration list so I can literally assign due dates to myself (or my team members can assign due dates to me) which helps to create those priorities. I fight this structure, but I recognize that I need it to move as quickly as I like to. When I wake up at 2:00 a.m. and add 13 things to the To Do lists, my EA jumps in at 6:00 a.m., develops her plan of attack and calls me with any questions she needs to talk through for more clarity or context before executing the initiatives.

As a sidebar, this applies to any of the people you lead. The social dynamics within our businesses have changed for the worst but that does not mean we have to accept it as "rule." I believe this short period of time will prove to be an exception in the otherwise powerful influence of business on the world. We can thrive. Do we want to stare at computers and talk to people down the hall through Zoom on a long-term basis? I do not think so because I do not think it is good for us as human beings. The human connection is the fuel that feeds business growth.

The Evolving Assistant

JOAN: *The secretary of yesterday is long gone. Even the Assistant of 2019 has evolved into a much more confident, assertive, "owner" mindset leader. During 2020, the Assistants were the ones taking the lead in getting offices packed up, helping employees set up in their homes, securing the necessary equipment, working with IT, learning and mastering virtual connecting tools, and navigating their Executive's calendars.*

EA Significance

Today's EA is smart, sharp, educated, and eager to make their leader shine. They have created massive networks with other assistants who they lean on for recommendations and best practices. They have built resiliency, adaptability, agility, and are pivot masters. They also learned how to become highly creative and took problem solving to a whole new level. This is the kind of partner you need to navigate the world and your busy life.

Blending of Your Personal and Professional Life

JOAN: *If you are like most people, you have moved away from the thought of a balanced lifestyle to a blending of your personal and professional life.*

EA Significance

A strategic EA partnership will make sure you are able to carve out your personal time and ensure you are able to get down to business when you need to. They will remind you of critical meetings and trips. It is not that they are going to manage your personal life unless they are a Personal Assistant. They are going to ensure you are achieving your goals.

SUMMARY
PART 2

James

- *Be prepared to pivot.*
- *The employee-employer relationship is at an end regarding formerly held work mores.*
- *These tech tools were created for the gaps when you cannot meet in person. They are not the solution for the long haul. We are social beings.*
- *We have learned that we can survive and thrive for periods of time because we are resilient.*
- *We can use tech tools to survive and maintain progress, but each tool presents one or more limitations that must be evaluated.*
- *We have to be cognizant that, no matter what, the relationship is better in person and apps can never fully replace that.*
- *Whenever possible, an Assistant and the Executive should meet in person to MAXIMIZE VALUE in the relationship.*
- *I cannot imagine what it would be like to lead businesses without a person committed and dedicated to supporting the initiatives, real time and in person with me.*
- *The human connection is the fuel that feeds business growth.*

YOUR COMPETITIVE EDGE

SUMMARY

PART 2

Joan

- *When a crisis strikes, we just get through it. We manage it. We do it.*
- *An EA can ensure the Executive stays connected ... even when they cannot be connected.*
- *Managers high in future-minded leadership skills have future-ready teams.*
- *The EA is the one who keeps the team connected and therefore able to remain in sync.*
- *Because your EA does the work they can do, it allows you the bandwidth necessary to do what only you can do.*
- *EAs have a spectacularly diverse and wide network of colleagues with specialized knowledge. If the EA does not know, they know someone who does!*
- *When an organization overloads an assistant with too many people to support, the assistant will suffer and so will the quality of their work.*
- *Your EA can help you maintain appropriate contact and help you decide when "in-person face time" is beneficial to your client, direct reports, and business objectives.*

GEMS
TO LEAD BY

PART 2

- A strategic EA partnership will make sure you are able to carve out your personal time and ensure you are able to get down to business when you need to.
- Not only will we survive this, but we will THRIVE through it.
- Be a servant leader who operates with vulnerability and authenticity.
- Be an approachable human.
- Leadership is about preparing for multiple possible futures along with the roadblocks and setbacks that may occur along the way.
- A great EA who acts as a Strategic Partner can help you to anticipate, forecast, and navigate the future.
- Stress tolerance is the threshold at which an individual can effectively and consistently deal with and manage stressful situations.

BUILDING A STRATEGIC PARTNERSHIP

A Wise Executive

JOAN: *He was way ahead of the times. In 1998, I was working with an Executive and asked him what he was looking for in an Executive Assistant. He specifically said, "I want a strategic business partner." I thought to myself, this Executive is brilliant! He saw his EA as much more than an order taker and task doer.*

My First Strategic Partnership:

At the young age of 24, I was fortunate to work for a very dynamic Executive, John, who was age 38, in a Fortune 500 company. John was brilliant, charismatic, well-respected, and a mover and shaker in the company. John taught me how to be his strategic partner. He taught me about business, how to work in tandem with him, how to execute his plan, how to command respect for my position as his right-hand person.

After two years, John moved into a newly created role within the company. From that point forward, I knew I always wanted a strategic partnership with my Executives.

The Three Stages of an Executive/EA Pairing
(As identified and created by Joan Burge)

The first stage is the most basic and almost everyone achieves this stage unless they have drastic personality or work style conflicts. At the onset of the team stage, the Executive/EA are learning to work together to accomplish daily tasks and complete projects. Within this stage, the partners grow to understand each other's work habits, communication style, general attitudes, beliefs, and get to know each other.

The second stage for an Executive/EA pairing is to develop a Star partnership. This stage encompasses knowing each other on a deeper level, such as understanding each other's work values, appreciating specific likes and dislikes, being curious and interested in the scope and depth of each other's jobs, working in concert, and seeing differences as assets versus liabilities to the team. At this level, the partners challenge each other's ideas, decisions, and processes.

The third stage for an Executive/EA pairing is a strategic partnership. Pay special attention to the word "strategic." This is the most fulfilling stage because it incorporates chemistry, shared values, and several other critical pairing aspects. At this level, the partners may describe themselves in some of the following ways:

- Two people who "click" despite their different views and opinions.
- Together, they can tackle anything
- Each is a part of the other's success
- If one becomes upset by something the other did, they are able to talk about it, settle it, and move beyond it, as a team
- It is thinking of the next step before the work partner tells them
- Knowing the next question, the partner is going to ask before they ask it
- When the unexpected arises–the partners confer on what to do about it
- The EA is considered "clairvoyant" by the leader

Joan Burge's Model: Stages of Growth for Executives & Assistants

(Note: While stage 3 is achieved by 30% of Executive/EA partnerships, stage 2 is a particularly good place to be. If you feel you are already at stage 2, I am certain you will have some revelations reading this book which will enhance your partnership with your EA.)

JOAN: *I like to use the analogy of a football game. In football, you have the players running the ball down the field. As an Executive Assistant, I can either be on the sidelines or in the stands cheering you on or I can run the ball down the field with you. I can block and I can tackle, too! Simply put, that is a strategic partnership between an Executive and the EA. Of course, to do that, I need to know a lot of things and we must have excellent communication.*

JAMES: *I love that analogy. I ask my EA to block for me all of the time, without even thinking about the reference to football! She can tackle,* *too, if I need her to play strong defense! It is really cool when we get to run the ball down the field together and make a touchdown, whether it's winning a new client, building key relationships with business stakeholders, hosting an annual company event, or working through a crisis.*

The Foundation for a Successful Partnership

A successful partnership with your EA starts with perceptions and expectations. What are your perceptions of your role in relation to your EA? What are your perceptions of an EA role? What are your perceptions of both of you as a team?

Expectations are tied to tasks. What tasks do you believe your EA should perform? What tasks should you perform? When expectations are not clearly stated or understood by work partners then job frustration, anger, resentment, and lack of motivation will result.

Understanding perceptions and defining expectations form and strengthen the foundation to build the partnership between you and your EA. Often, when Executives and Executive Assistants begin to work together, they do not begin by taking time to discuss what they expect and their views of each other's roles, beyond a written job description. As a result, the pairing may spend months struggling, wasting time, and misunderstanding each other, rather than building a stabilized partnership with a strong momentum that grows daily.

In many organizations, when a new leader joins the organization or is moved from one department/division to another, the leader will inherit the incumbent Executive Assistant. It could even possibly be a relationship that neither one would have chosen through an interviewing process!

Perceptions are as important as expectations. Even if you have been working with your current EA for a long time, it is never too late for clarification. <u>Remember, people are not static.</u> People do not remain unchanged year after year! They develop over time, shaped by input from events, occurrences, successes, and failures, both personal and professional.

JOAN: *If I were providing you and your assistant with personal coaching in the area of perceptions and expectations, here is what I would tell you:*

> *"We live in an age of rapid technology shifts and instant gratification. The new knowledge economy in which we work demands almost instantaneous, intuitive moves to jump ahead of the competition.*
>
> *I cannot emphasize more clearly this critical moment within our world than this: Talking with your Executive Assistant about perceptions and expectations may uncover some new interests about each other that will enhance the team pairing relationship. And that will be the intuitive move that allows you to jump ahead. This will provide you with a Competitive Edge."*

How To Create a Strategic Partnership

JOAN: *Creating a strategic partnership takes time. We have to learn about each other, the business, our likes and dislikes, what works and what doesn't work, and much more. Our best advice is to be patient. It is well worth the effort. I will also say, from my own experience, some of my strategic partnerships grew quickly because we had great chemistry, similar values, and work styles.*

Keep in mind this important fact: strategic partnership is not a place where you arrive, and you are done! Executive/EA strategic partnerships are constantly evolving. That is because:

- *People change.*
- *The business changes.*
- *Expectations change.*
- *Strategic partners are on a journey of continuous improvement.*
- *Each person grows and takes on new assignments.*
- *Obstacles present themselves and opportunities to better the business and each other.*
- *Emerging technologies, advancements, crises, and industry trends all cause the Executive/EA team to pivot.*

Building a strategic partner with your EA starts with a desire, especially on your part. I know several Executive Assistants (and that is an understatement!) who want to have a strategic partnership with their leader. You have to want this—want to experience the benefits of this type of work relationship. Then comes commitment and discipline.

Being in Agreement
(Excerpt from Joan Burge's *Executives & Assistants Working in Partnership: The Definitive Guide*)

It is important that, from the outset of this growth and development process, both parties are clear and agree upon some basic points regarding the partnership.

Consider documenting these points into what will become a valuable agreement. Together, you can design its contents. Ultimately, both the Executive and the Executive Assistant should seek alignment from the very beginning on the key fundamental points presented in the document. We also recommend revisiting this document regularly (several times a year) to ensure it still feels accurate and meaningful.

Define the Goals of the Partnership

What is the purpose of this pairing? Establish an empowering statement that articulates exactly what you want this partnership to be and what kind of results you want to achieve. To help your thought process, here are some key descriptors/phrases you may wish to include:

- Mutually supportive.
- Mutually beneficial.
- Each person contributes fully.
- We each leverage and build upon our unique strengths.
- We compensate for one another's weaknesses.
- We create more value together.
- We make one another more effective.

You may choose to be more detailed and establish specific long-term, mid-term, or even short-term, goals. But remember: This is not a vast list of business goals; these are the goals of the partnership.

Define the Role(s) of Each Partner

What is each person's unique position in this partnership? This is not a job description so do not get too granular in describing responsibilities. This is simply a high-level look at what each person brings to the relationship.

For the Executive's role, consider using words such as:

- Guide
- Mentor

- Coach
- Advise
- Inform
- Inspire

For the EA's role, consider using words such as:
- Protect
- Communicate
- Listen
- Filter/Shield
- Organize
- Coach/Mentor
- Manage
- Solve
- Block and Tackle

Identify Advantageous Behaviors

Finally, define the advantageous behaviors you agree to utilize in creating this kind of partnership. Once again, keep this high-level. We will talk about specific process-related behaviors and best practices later. For now, focus on identifying behaviors that will cultivate the relationship. Here are some of the advantageous behaviors we recommend:

Remember: You Are Both Human

It is important that you know and understand each other as real people. Discuss your strengths and weaknesses openly. Be sensitive when your work partner is going through a rough time, either personally or professionally. When you pay attention to each other and the ups and downs that are bound to occur, you are better able to navigate the day-to-day demands in the workplace. You compensate for one another—the Executive Assistant supporting the Executive and even the other way around on occasion.

Genuinely Care

When you truly care about each other as people and care about each other's successes, your working relationship will flourish. Take time to visit with each other and touch base on the personal side of life. Ask about the kids, weekend plans, and about favorite outside-of-work pastimes.

In a truly powerful partnership, you even know when your work partner is nervous about an upcoming medical procedure or ill spouse. The details of life, within reason, matter. When something is important and taking up valuable real estate in your mind, sharing a small bit of information with your partner is appropriate and will help them better understand your frame of mind.

Being "friendly" at work doesn't mean you have to be "friends." Most people prefer to have boundaries between home-life and work-life. Respect each other's boundaries, but do not be so rigid that you come off as robotic and lifeless. Show empathy, listen, and learn to care for each other as people, not just work partners.

Value and Respect Each Other

Unfortunately, in my experience, many Executive Assistants do not feel valued. They frequently feel brushed aside when someone else enters the room. Their Executives do not make time for them; they do not offer the EA praise and are not open to their ideas. Executive Assistants often feel they are second behind everyone else on the team.

Respect is a two-way street. Each partner provides value, and each deserves respect. This is shown in the amount of time you spend together, how you communicate with and care about one another, and how you generally treat each other.

Your interactions are a demonstration—to each other as well as to those around you—of your mutual respect or lack of it.

Build Exceptional Levels of Trust

Trust is also a two-way street. It is the absolute foundation upon which strong partnerships are built.

An Executive Assistant wants to know the Executive will support them. An Executive has to trust the Executive Assistant with a multitude of important information and assignments, and trust that the EA will do a good job and not let anything fall through the cracks.

Realize that you are dependent on each other. An Executive Assistant relies on the Executive to provide direction, information, and inspiration. An Executive depends on the EA to completely follow through on assignments, tasks, and projects. Both parties must uphold their end of the bargain to achieve success.

Depending on each other also means holding each other accountable, keeping your partner focused, and tactfully telling your partner if they are out of line or have crossed the line.

Be Willing To Have Uncomfortable Conversations

Constructive feedback can be hard to hear and hard to deliver. No one enjoys the process, but too many Executive/EA partners avoid it.

The Executive Assistant needs to give the Executive important feedback, but instead, sweeps it under the rug.

The Executive needs to tell the EA they lack a certain level of polish or professionalism, but instead, suppresses the information.

The issues do not go away, they are diverted. They either come out in different, more passive, and indirect ways, or they turn into resentments. Whatever the case, the outcome is unproductive, and the problem does not get resolved; it only deteriorates the partnership and the ability of the individual to be a stronger contributor.

Executives and Executive Assistants must both be able to have necessary conversations to improve individual performance and/or team performance. Both parties must learn to be tactful, considerate, and professional in their approach. The key is not to ignore the difficult conversations. Facing them head on can often create an immediate deeper bond in the partnership.

In summary, BOTH parties need to be able to feel safe enough to give thoughtful, honest feedback with the intent to build stronger, better teaming. And the Executive should be open to feedback, too. For starters, you may wish to ask your EA if there is something you should begin doing or stop doing or are there roadblocks you can remove to help the EA in their work.

With that said, here are some ideas to get you started so you can then implement the ideas in this book:

Realize You Are Dependent on Each Other To Achieve Results

Of course, an Executive depends on their Executive Assistant to get things done. What is more important to understand is that your EA depends on you to provide clear direction, clarify your expectations, give them the work in a timely fashion (not always last minute), support them, check in with them, and involve them in the scope of your work.

Communicate, Communicate, Communicate!

Communication comes from the Latin word communis, meaning common. When we communicate, we are trying to establish "commonness" with someone. We are trying to share information, an idea, an attitude, or trying to comprehend what someone is sharing with us.

Communication is like a huge umbrella that covers and affects all that goes on between human beings. Communication is a strong factor in deciding what kind of relationship a person has with others. You must have ready at hand the quality of communication that operates smoothly and efficiently wherever you are, whatever issues you encounter. Why? Because every day you will interact with other people. You cannot pull out a broken communication tool or discover you misplaced your tact or diplomacy somewhere! And if you lose your temper, you will communicate "wrong side up and wrong side out" and become soaked in the process! To not invest in communication skills is to limit your ideas and image so completely that it is like shielding yourself with wet newspaper on a rainy day ... useless.

Communication is complex; rarely will you find it black and white. You will not learn everything about it in one day ... and you will always need additional growth in this area.

Work partners face demanding schedules every day, with their own lists of priorities, tasks, and projects to do. The Executive Assistant not only has a list of tasks and projects, but also has the multitude of work generated by their leader. It is easy for days and even weeks to pass without the team having intentional and purposeful communication. As a result, projects fall through the cracks; work has to be redone because it wasn't first clarified, stress can build, and disappointment sets in.

Not all communication is created equal. Be rigorous in your standards to avoid the common challenges that block communication.

To do this, keep the following in mind.

- Email is NOT the best medium for all communication. Nothing gets to the heart of the matter as quickly and effectively as face-to-face communication. When that is not possible, picking up the phone and speaking in real time will often get the point across much faster and with more clarity than an endless communication back and forth via email.

- Two-way communication requires active participation on both sides. This means listening as well as speaking. Listening happens with your eyes, mind, and heart, not just your ears. Manage distractions when communicating; multi-tasking wastes time and increases the likelihood of miscommunication.

- Communication takes time. Every minute spent communicating now will save you ten down the road. It is an investment that yields exponential returns. But there is no substitute for putting in the time. Allow for informal, quick, spur-of-the-moment discussions to unfold naturally throughout the day. Also, block time on the calendar for regular meetings with a set agenda and keep these appointments.

Model Other Great Leaders

Leaders who understand the Executive/EA partnership employ these best practices:

- Mentor the EA.
- Communicate on a regular basis.

- Include the EA in leadership meetings and Executive retreats.
- Forward industry articles, blogs, newsletters, and magazines on industry or workplace trends to their EA, so they can keep pace with the Executive.
- Communicate big picture as well as details.
- Co-partner.
- Include EA in decision making.
- Listen with understanding.
- Include EA in goal setting.
- Co-develop EA's career path by fostering professional growth.
- Share information with the EA in a timely manner.
- Respect personality differences.
- Understand when the EA may be having a rough day.
- Are open to addressing opportunities to improve.
- Show they care about their EA as a person.

Become Champions of Change

JOAN: *I recognize that developing this kind of highly communicative, trusting partnership between Executive and EA may be outside the norm in your organization. While change of any sort is difficult for those involved, it is also inspiring for those on the outside. I encourage you to view yourselves as Champions of Change. You are leading the way for others to improve their partnerships as well. Through your positive actions, others will grow eager to act themselves.*

Focus on your own success and recognize that you may also be working to create a new standard for others. It is no exaggeration to say that I have seen entire organizational cultures shift in the wake of such improvements. When one area improves, it often shines a light on others where work is still needed.

Remember that change can also create resistance. Watch for this in yourself and others. Your commitment to the end goal is essential. This is a worthwhile process, the results of which will quickly be evident to you and those around you.

When you work to build a strategic partnership with your EA you will achieve a brilliant facet of the Competitive Edge.

SUMMARY

PART 3

James

- *Ask your EA to block for you.*
- *It is really cool when an Executive and EA get to run the ball down the field together and make a touchdown.*

SUMMARY

PART 3

Joan

- *Your interactions are a demonstration—to each other as well as to those around you—of your mutual respect or lack of it.*
- *When something is important and taking up valuable real estate in your mind, sharing a small bit of information with your partner is appropriate and will help them better understand your frame of mind.*
- *Being "friendly" at work doesn't mean you have to be "friends."*
- *Be willing to have uncomfortable conversations.*
- *To not invest in communication skills is to limit your ideas and image so completely that it is like shielding yourself with wet newspaper on a rainy day ... useless.*
- *Every minute spent communicating now will save you ten down the road.*

GEMS TO LEAD BY

PART 3

- Teach your EA how to execute your plan, how to command respect for their position as your right-hand person.
- The third stage of partnership is the most fulfilling stage because it incorporates chemistry, shared values, and synergizing teamwork.
- A successful partnership with your EA starts with perceptions and expectations.
- People are not static.
- Work to build exceptional levels of trust.
- When we communicate, we are trying to establish "commonness" with someone.
- When you truly care about each other as people and care about each other's successes, your working relationship will flourish.
- Facing feedback head-on can often create an immediate deeper bond in the partnership.
- Realize you are dependent on each other to achieve results.

HOW TO MAXIMIZE THE TIME & TALENTS OF AN EXECUTIVE ASSISTANT

Benefits of Leveraging Your Executive Assistant's Skills

With the demands placed upon Executives in today's competitive business environment and the tectonic shifts discussed earlier, a greater need exists for Executives to use the time and talents of their Executive Assistant. A fully utilized EA helps to facilitate the Executive's job, sets the tone for the office, is seen as the channel of communication, and can be a center of influence.

JOAN: *Even back in 1970 when I became an EA, there has always been a need for leaders to fully utilize their Executive Assistant by leveraging their talents and maximizing their time. I believe there is a much stronger need now because many leaders are independent and tech savvy. And organizations are working lean, forcing EAs to support multiple Executives.*

Executives do not fully utilize the talents of an EA for some commonly stated reasons, such as:

- *They do not understand what an EA is capable of doing. The scope of the role has expanded tremendously. There are intricacies to the role that most people do not see.*
- *There is hesitation on the Executive's side because they do not know if they can or should delegate a certain task. It is not that they are thinking of personal tasks, they just are not sure what they could ask even in relation to business.*
- *Another scenario is when an Executive never had an outstanding EA before, so they think a mediocre EA is the norm.*

I always say, "If you have never eaten in a 5-star restaurant, you think a 3-star restaurant is great. Or if you have never stayed at a 5-star hotel, you think a 3-star hotel is wonderful." You do not know what you do not know.

Changing Perceptions

Aside from communicating honestly, openly, and consistently regarding expectations and perceptions around the role, communication is required to keep the constant stream of information flowing back and forth between Executive and EA, and from the EA to other parties. As one CEO of a Fortune 500 company told Joan Burge in an interview, "Administrative assistants are the center of influence." He described his assistant as a "flow manager," meaning she helped facilitate progress. She had the power to keep things moving at an optimal pace. Utilizing the EA as a "center of influence" means everything flows through the Executive Assistant. Your EA becomes the central hub through which all information, strategies, goals, objectives, planning, communications, and such will flow.

Today's Executive Receives Information Via...

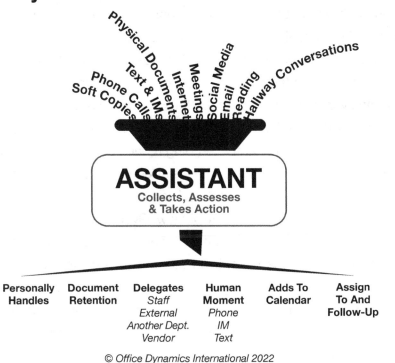

Personally Handles	Document Retention	Delegates	Human Moment	Adds To Calendar	Assign To And Follow-Up
		Staff	*Phone*		
		External	*IM*		
		Another Dept.	*Text*		
		Vendor			

© Office Dynamics International 2022

Executives receive information from many different sources. You are having hallway conversations, you are texting, having meet ups at Starbucks, having phone conversations while walking through the airport or while commuting, or in down-time opportunities, you are doing research, so you have all this data swirling out there in a foggy cloud around your position. These various data points and communications come to you, but your EA gets only a little piece of it. How well can that EA really help you? If you funnel action items and information or at least copy your EA on emails, then your EA can truly assist as your partner. Remember the earlier football analogy of running the ball down the field together? It is hard to be a successful receiver when the quarterback never releases the ball.

Some Executives resist this concept. Executives are independent and many are proud of it. They certainly can manage many of these items on their own, but should they? Is that where their attention rightly belongs? In some cases, they add confusion and overlap by being involved in things their EA should be managing. It can even create embarrassment when it becomes clear to others that the Executive and EA are not on the same page working in tandem as a team. By allowing everything to flow through the Executive Assistant, the Executive leverages the EA as a buffer or filter—a conduit for collecting information, processing it, and sending it back out in the appropriate fashion. It frees the Executive to focus attention where it is needed. It allows the EA to truly be involved in all aspects of the Executive's business, giving a more holistic point-of-view. Over time, the EA develops the ability to anticipate needs and truly act as an "alter ego" for the Executive. Utilizing the Executive Assistant as a center of influence requires a deep level of continual communication by and between both parties. The Executive must freely and promptly share information. The Executive Assistant must clearly and accurately do the same. This concept creates deep interdependence between them.

At the beginning of the Executive/EA relationship, the initial formation requires some understanding that when something is delegated, it will be taken care of accurately and promptly. That takes trust. Trust builds over time. Initially, it is not natural to delegate when you are a leader. Many times, we are just used to doing it ourselves and it will be done to our liking when we do it ourselves. Like training anybody, when you train the EA to do it to your liking eventually, they become an extension of you.

The Executive Assistant as an Information Flow Manager

JAMES: *International travel in the "old days" had to be so peaceful. Just jump on a plane and disconnect. No Wi-Fi, no email, no texting. I would love an eight-hour airplane ride free of phone, text messages, or email. I am also thinking about how peaceful it would be to just "be me," alone in my thoughts for eight hours.*

- *How much more organized could I be?*
- *How much more tangible work would get done?*
- *What deep concentration detail work could I do on a flight where I did not have any of those interruptions.*

But for some people, being disconnected for eight hours during a workday would be emotionally damaging!

I think we have more volume going into the funnel referred to earlier, and the funnel is shorter. I do not have a long funnel that allows for time for the EA to filter through it and for me as the Executive to provide that information and sort it out.

We are getting dumped with information at a faster rate. I do not know that it is more information, but it is at a faster rate, and it is the expectation that it comes out of the bottom of the funnel at a much faster rate.

JOAN: *My work requires me to have a lot of quiet, uninterrupted time because of all the writing I do. I write our courses, webinar scripts, my speeches, books, blog content, and more. I have a small team. My needs are very different than James. Pre-COVID, I traveled often to teach onsite classes. The great part of that was I had lots of time on an airplane where I could write to my heart's content. I did not stay connected on purpose. I left that to my EA. My EA checked my emails. If there was something urgent, she would let me know when I landed. Personally, I love not always being connected. My brain is not task switching constantly, which means I get a lot of work done with concentrated focus, thus producing a better result. This provides me quality thinking time. I have got my rhythm going and I am on fire!*

A Creative Solution To Provide Focused Time

JOAN: *This is something I used to do for my Executives. Have your Executive Assistant schedule a meeting for you with yourself. This could be a few days a week at a certain time of day. For example, I have a meeting with Joan (myself) at 4:00 p.m. every day. That is so I can wrap up any loose ends from the day, get ready for the next day or next few days, return unimportant calls, review P&Ls, and scroll through my email to see if I missed anything, etc.*

This does not mean I will not have something interrupt my meeting with myself at the last-minute. Try it ... you might like it!

JOAN: *I realize everyone struggles with time today, especially Executives who are accessible by people who can privately message them on Facebook, LinkedIn, and What's App. As an Executive, you may feel like you want to say, "Leave me alone! I have stuff to do!"*

JAMES: *I think this might be one spot where we are going to disagree with regard to where it is headed. I acknowledge that it is extremely difficult to not respond or want to respond quickly. I believe the reason is because those actions, that responsiveness, that accessibility, that "stick-to-it and doing it faster than everybody else around you" is how young Executives grow quickly in their positions.*

There is no way I would be the CEO of our organization or president of our organization if I couldn't run faster than my peers; if I wasn't the first to respond; the one who rolled out of bed at three in the morning and the one who stayed until 10:00 o'clock at night; if I didn't respond to those emails, get the data to where it needed to be, take care of those clients as fast as I have, I know for a fact that I wouldn't have been as successful as I am today. It is because everybody around you is trying to run at that same pace.

Blending Both Worlds

JOAN: *I am not saying to not be responsive. There are many times I answer a text on my own or respond to a private message. I flow the majority of things through Melia because she can handle it from that point forward. Know when you need to loop your EA in even if you responded yourself, but then maybe that is when in your huddle you would tell them, "Hey, I got a text this morning from someone so here's what's going on." Boom.*

JAMES: *It is recognizing, first and foremost, that there is more than one way to get it done and some of the tried-and-true principles of business, like slow down to go fast still work but perhaps not every time. I would hate to have a strategic partner who was just like me. I want an EA strategic partner that balances me out and has the strengths where my weaknesses are; my weaknesses become their strengths.*

Recognizing that if I am going to go fast, and I am going to sprint, and I am going to be overly accessible, and I am going to log into Wi-Fi on the airplane on an international trip, my EA strategic partner is going to need to be the type of person who slows me down intentionally with permission.

JOAN: *If you are an Executive who is more comfortable not having that accessibility, not having the cell phone in your hand all the time, you would not need the same kind of EA strategic partner as James. If you condition yourself for the huddle, it is just like when you condition yourself for other things that matter to you. How many Executives go to the gym every morning? They are conditioned for it, and they will get up at 5:00 a.m. to make it happen. I just ask that Executives give conditioning for the huddle a try for a few weeks. I think they would find great value in doing so.*

I want to speak from an Executive Assistant's perspective. The value I give when I am in the office with you, when you are there, even if you are running off to meetings, is immense. I am a savvy EA; I am picking up on your body language. I am watching your facial expressions. I am sensing your sense of urgency. I am noticing your hot buttons. I know what excites you because I see it. Imagine how much more I could help you? When I was an EA, I listened to my Executives' conversations. That is how I learned, how I picked up on things, and how I could anticipate what was going to happen next.

When things are really tough, and I am struggling, I am not sleeping at night, and stuff is going on in my personal life, it is still my job to come in as the CEO and pump up my team and say, "Go team! We are going to do this. We are going to thrive in this." Your EA can mirror that language and the tone. You may also want to set a tone of, "Hey, quit messing around! We have got this big presentation coming up, heads down, and engage yourself."

The Art of Delegation

This brings us to the topic of delegation. You are going to have to delegate to your EA partner. That is easier said than done. Let us look at the barriers and benefits to delegation, how to grow trust through delegation, deciding which tasks to assign to your Executive Assistant, and how to initiate delegating with confidence.

Barriers to Delegation

Before we address what to delegate, let us look at why Executives do not delegate certain tasks or assignments to their EA.

JOAN: *Here are some reasons I have heard over the years from Executives who did not want or know how to properly delegate work to their EA:*

- *"I am a perfectionist."*
- *"I have had bad past experiences with other EAs."*
- *"My current EA has let me down."*
- *"I do not even think about delegating because I am busy doing the task."*
- *"I am too busy to turn it over properly."*
- *"I am not sure what I can delegate to my EA."*

Delegate More

There are some great Executives who are delegating but it seems like that might just stop at a certain scope of tasks. They are not grasping that they could assign more projects or tasks to their EA.

JAMES: *I do not know that it is just the Executive's fault for not delegating. I think the relationship has to be one where the EA is continually challenging the Executive to delegate more. I find that I will dump as much work as I think my EA can handle, and if she doesn't reply to me, "Give me more, I need more!" then I'm going to assume she's got her hands full. If I do not see her or hear from her other than during our daily huddle, I am going to assume she is busy working on the assigned tasks on her list. If my EA comes back to me and says, "You gave me four hours' worth of work; I still have four hours of open time," then I am going to load her up!*

JOAN: *For over four decades the primary reason I have heard as to why Executives do not delegate is they are not really sure what to delegate to their Executive Assistant. I have had managers learning how to work with their EA through a workshop or in coaching ask, "Can I really ask my EA to write that thank-you note on my behalf? That is personal. Shouldn't I really be doing that?" Or "Can I ask my EA to order flowers for my partner?"*

There are certain things I know you can ask an EA to do for you. Other things like booking your family vacation, buying a gift for your spouse, or managing your second home, are up for discussion. Some EAs have no problem doing any of these items. They view it as whatever makes their Executive's life easier they will do, and are usually well compensated for it. Other Assistants feel you are infringing.

JAMES: *I have seen this uncertainty, too, "Am I really allowed to ask my Executive Assistant to do that?" It is not always personal stuff, but sometimes it is professional tasks that seem like they should be done by the Executive themselves. For example, it could be a simple yet meaningful task, like preparing a thank-you note for a great client. Shouldn't I write those myself? Or what about preparation of the proposals and contracts for new clients? For each of these examples, I held onto the tasks for far too long. For client thank-you cards, I dictate the messages to my EA who writes in all block letters, like I do, and then I sign the cards. She prepares the envelopes and ensures the cards are sent out when appropriate. She even prepares cards when I have not thought to do it. When I started my first business, I prepared every proposal and all client contracts. Then I realized that I have hired brilliant people who can perform this task to my liking and as needed for the business IF I get out of their way and simply teach them how to do it and put in a few exceptions that I am most concerned with (dollar value, service quality risk, etc.). Being able to perform a task yourself is powerful, but the issue with doing it yourself EVERY TIME is that you must do it EVERY TIME.*

As Executives, we must recognize that the relationship between Executive and Executive Assistant is that of a mentor/mentee relationship. Rather than a patriarchal (old school style) relationship, it should be more like an "older sibling" style. As the Executive, aside from needing to delegate for the sake of effectiveness in your position, you need to do it for the sake of your commitment to your Executive Assistant's professional development. So, what can you expect to happen? The first time you teach your EA how to do something, it takes ten times longer than if you just did it yourself. The second time it takes eight times longer, the third time five times longer, and your goal is to get to a point where it is significantly more efficient to have your EA do it, and often, the quality is better than if you had done it yourself. This takes intentional effort and direction, founded on the value of the strategic partnership.

If you have made the commitment to your Executive Assistant that you are going to have a strategic partnership, they are going to have a mutually beneficial outcome with you and they want you to succeed just like you want them to succeed. Once you have that, then you have to trust in the process and make it happen.

The Benefits of Delegating

JOAN: *Aside from saving an Executive time and energy, there is another set of eyes looking at that particular item. When I delegate something to my Executive Assistant, Melia, she will methodically take the time to look at that item I initiated and really massage it. Melia will come up with things I did not think of, or she will come back to me and say, "Did you really mean to say this? Or do this?" This is a huge benefit, especially when I am moving so quickly.*

It is absolutely critical to have that kind of relationship with your EA. When they are comfortable in their role, they should be able to challenge you in your way of thinking or your way of doing things. For example, if you are writing a client letter from a template that you have used before and it took you two hours to develop the template and you turn that task over to your EA, they can start with your template and the strategy that you have outlined for your desired outcome. They can massage it and improve it. Instead of you spending two hours on that task, you get to come back to it after they have spent two hours on it. Likely it is better than it was in the template, and you get to spend 15 minutes on it and make it 5 or 10% better yet.

By bringing your EA into those tasks and encouraging them to be your partner through delegation, you get to spend less time at a higher value for the sake of constant improvement. If I just use the same template every single time,

- *the quality of work does not increase.*
- *the quality of my message does not increase.*
- *the overall effectiveness of my office does not improve.*

Another great reason why we delegate is that an EA knows who is who. They know players. They have all these different connections. They have their network they could go to if they do not have the answer, or they need additional information or backup. They are very resourceful and that is of supremely high value.

JAMES: *My Executive Assistant frequently reaches out to the Executive Assistants of other Executives within my network. When I am collaborating with another Executive, it is nice to have my EA also collaborating with that Executive's EA at a different level where they are working together strategically on a foundation of something even while the Executive and I are working on a vision. You get this exponential impact rather than a linear impact.*

I love that you could have this one-on-one ratio, which is a straight line on a graph. This scenario, where I work on something, then my EA works on it, creates limited and linear effectiveness. The benefit your discussing is exponential, so when I work on it and concurrently my EA works on it, we achieve

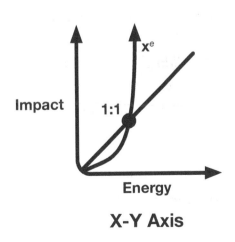

a Competitive Edge and impact to the 10th power! Rather than a linear function, the effectiveness of that concurrent work ends up being logarithmically greater! That is one of the most important elements of effective delegation.

JOAN: *When I was an EA, I liked to be delegated to. I wanted to grow. I wanted to be challenged. I wanted to be my executive's partner. The only way I could learn how to be their partner was for them to bring me into their world.*

JAMES: *It is a partnership that should be taken extremely seriously. The training and development of that relationship needs to be one of the most important components of an Executive's day because it represents who they are as an Executive.*

It is important for an EA to be aligned with the Executive from a ...
- *Messaging perspective.*
- *Vision perspective.*
- *Goals perspective.*

Without that alignment, there is nothing to train to, there is no direction to train for. Once that vision and alignment are established, it is just a matter of building that relationship, building that trust, delegating, and then instituting a feedback loop.

Information and vision travels from the Executive to the

A fully utilized Executive Assistant helps facilitate the Executive's job, sets the tone for the office, is seen as the channel of communication, and can be a center of influence.

Executive Assistant and then it has to loop back through the network returning to the Executive. The Executive can adjust the message or the training or the goal, and send it back to the EA. You get this constant loop of process improvement if it starts with a strong relationship between the Executive and Executive Assistant. It is going to radiate to everyone within that network and now you have really accelerated that impact.

Delegation Requires Trust

JAMES: *Trust is the foundation of the Executive-EA relationship, and you should build trust in those relationships over time so that they can continue to flourish. Stephen Covey authored a book called, The Speed of Trust: The One Thing That Changes Everything. In that book, there are many references to methods for developing trusting partnerships and trustworthy relationships quickly, to create efficiency and speed within the business arena. In many organizations, trust builds more quickly with an EA than other team members, primarily because you work so much more closely with your EA. I have one-on-one meetings with my direct reports on a regular weekly basis. I meet almost daily with my EA. Most of the time, the meetings with my EA are shorter and more of a daily huddle, where we are talking about what we have going on in the short term and how it is driving our initiatives forward. When I meet with my direct reports, the conversations are more focused on their goals and initiatives. I tend to stay out of the weeds and not tell them what to do, but instead, ask a lot of open-ended questions to promote thought and focus. By keeping the meeting frequency to no more than weekly, I keep myself from becoming micro-managerial and thus, maintain trust within those relationships.*

When we talk about trust from an Executive's perspective, they want to trust that their EA will:

- *Keep confidential information private.*
- *Follow-through on assignments, tasks, timelines, to do lists with minimal or no follow-up.*
- *Make sound decisions in a manner consistent with the Executive's expectations.*
- *Represent the Executive in a way they want to be represented.*

The Cycle of Trust: Most Executive-EA relationships begin with an absence of trust altogether. An Executive must turn over work or assignments to their EA and give them a chance to earn trust. As that EA proves themselves, the Executive will be inclined to turn over more work to the EA. And not just more work, but eventually, this will morph into mission-critical assignments. Do not assume your EA will always get it right the first time, 100% of the time, especially if it is something new. Yes, the basics like calendaring and travel should be a given for the job description, but over time and as trust builds, the EA should become an extension of the Executive. This is also how the relationship grows into a strategic partnership.

From Joan's and James' experiences, it can take as much as 6-12 months of building the foundation for a trusting relationship to develop between an Executive and an EA. From a job perspective, it takes about one year for an EA to see the full cycle of your business and industry, so this is where you want to give some wiggle room. At the 12-month mark, you should have a strong indication that your EA can become a strategic partner in the future. As long as you see an upward trajectory of your EA's understanding, you are on track and should continue to discuss the path, challenge your EA to grow, and push more critical initiatives to your EA for execution.

JAMES: Tips To Accelerate Trust Building With Your Executive Assistant

1. *Have your EA meet with your direct reports to learn about you. Then, ask your EA to interview you with that information in hand to help them dig deeper into getting to know you and your work style.*

2. *Ask your EA to write a letter on your behalf. Then sit down with the EA and edit it together, to go through the bits and pieces that are and are not your style. This gives them constructive feedback on how to write like you do.*

3. *Share professional failures or "what you'd do differently next time" with your EA. It helps to provide context as the EA is learning to manage the relationship with you and to grasp the history and lessons learned.*

4. *Within the first few months, regularly ask "How would you resolve this issue if it were solely up to you?" Then if it is different than your thinking, ask yourself, "Is this acceptable or good enough?" If it is good enough but different than how you would do it, share how you would resolve/handle but use the EA's proposed solution.*

5. *Within the first few months when the EA does something that is not how you want it to be done, have a direct conversation. Do not be evasive, indirect, soft or coy about it. This is your opportunity to build their knowledge base and subject matter expertise, not to mention build trust deeper into the relationship.*

6. *Meet with your EA regularly. Ensure that some of the meetings are for your EA's professional development and not just huddles regarding your agenda or initiatives.*

7. *Make sure that most, if not all, of your meetings are in-person. The sterility of virtual meetings is detrimental to the trust-building process.*

8. *Do what you say you are going to do. Be transparent about your short-comings, strengths, etc. and ask for help in the areas you need it most. Then follow through on what you commit to. It seems odd to write this to Executives, but frankly, CEOs do not have many people holding them accountable to their action items.*

Deciding Which Tasks To Assign to Your Executive Assistant

Deciding which tasks to assign to your Executive Assistant can feel overwhelming, especially if you have never had an EA. Even if you have had an EA for several years, you still may be missing golden opportunities to hand off tasks, projects, client relations, and so much more.

JOAN: *In my coaching work and private conversations with Executives, they often will ask if it is okay to delegate "X" to their Executive Assistant. Usually, my answer is a resounding "Yes." The list of what to delegate can be a long one. Instead, I am providing questions specific to delegation to guide you. Then, I will provide a brief checklist of delegation ideas.*

Does my Executive Assistant have the innate ability/talent?

JOAN: *All of us have innate talents. Intentionally look for and analyze your EA's strengths. Does your EA excel in the following?*

- *Managing projects*
- *Writing concisely or writing with impact*
- *Being persuasive*
- *Organizational skills*
- *Looking for and identifying details*
- *Creativity (we do not mean graphic design)*
- *Presenting abstract ideas*
- *Seeing the big picture*
- *People skills*
- *Being a great listener*
- *Anticipating outcomes and the future*
- *Being methodical*

Identify those strengths. Then push out assignments, projects, and tasks that leverage those talents. Your EA will do a great job, resulting in you both being happy.

JAMES: *I believe an Executive needs to decide if they need an Executive Assistant who is complementary or supplementary to their own skill set. Supplementary means that the EA has a similar skill set which, when paired with the Executive's, will enlarge the depth of the Executive's influence. Complementary means that the EA has a completely different set of skills, which will expand the breadth of the Executive's effectiveness.*

Due to my servant leadership style paired with a visionary (low detail) approach, I personally prefer a complementary EA, so that I can reduce the impact of my weaknesses. I intentionally look for Executive Assistants and partners in business that have business styles that are different than my own. Usually, they have a different perspective on life, a unique set of skills, and a different way of getting things done. When you have selected a complementary EA relationship, you will likely find that there are innate skills they have that you simply don't have, and you value them due to your lack in that area. From that uniqueness and complementary role, there will naturally be a certain set of tasks or roles that automatically become theirs because they are automatically better to deal with it than you are.

I tend to be a visionary, thinking at the 30,000-foot elevation level. I am uber strategic. I like to solve puzzles. I like to get very abstract and think things through five, six, and seven steps down the road. I like the game of "what if." I recognize that while I am in that space, a whole bunch of really important tasks that are highly detailed and very important at the ground level are being overlooked.

My Executive Assistant, Kayla, is the exact opposite. She is here and now. Kayla is very detailed-oriented. She is tangible in the sense that she does not really want to deal with the abstract world. We have an understanding that if I start migrating into that abstract space, Kayla just lets me go off on a tangent.

We also have an understanding that while I am out there, she is going to focus on the things that I am forgetting to deal with. These could be things like birthdays, new employees that need my attention, or executing a contract that needs to be dealt with today.

Does my EA have experience in a particular area that I do not know about?

JOAN: *This is an important question. Often the skills that people utilize in their personal life can be transferred to their professional life. When I was a young working mother and wife, I also did volunteer work and was active on charitable committees or chaired fundraisers. What skills do you think I needed to do those things?*

- *Hyper-organized*
- *Focus*
- *Manage time extremely well*
- *Juggle multiple complex calendars and deadlines*
- *Employ excellent communication skills*
- *Ability to wear a variety of hats and play a variety of roles*
- *Leadership*
- *Put out last-minute fires*
- *Persuasion*
- *Planning*
- *Interpersonal strength*
- *Teamwork*

Every one of those skills and abilities transferred to my role of being a strategic partner to top Executives.

JAMES: *I do not know that we even need to limit it to the things that we do not know about. Just because something is listed on a resume does not necessarily explain the depth of their understanding about a skill or the depth of knowledge on the topic. When I hired Kayla there was a snippet on her resume about some experience with a specific financial accounting software. A year after our relationship started, I joined an organization that wanted to use that software. I ended up becoming the Executive champion for the initiative for a* *substantial division and was in way over my head with the software integration. As soon as I started to share the strategy and the objectives from a leadership perspective with my Executive Assistant, she told me she had substantial experience in that arena, reminding me she had put it on her resume. She became the Executive champion from my office, and we were successful with the initiative and shared in the glory of conquering the challenge together.*

JOAN: *Going back to Jasmine who was my first real EA strategic partner, after I saw what she could manage I started pushing more and more her way. But it was not just busy work. I had Jasmine join me in my Facebook Lives, she ventured into managing our social media, hosted educational coffee chats, emceed our conferences. As my work expanded and the business grew, I expected her to take on more, and I made sure I gave her those opportunities. I have used the same practice with Melia who has been with me since 2016. Melia has grown in other ways and taken on different roles and responsibilities than Jasmine did because our company looks different today.*

JAMES: *What comes to my mind is that you were at a point in your career where you were growing, you were challenging yourself with new content, and as that occurred you looked at your workload and said, "I need some help. I need to take more things off my plate." Who did you turn to? Your Executive Assistant strategic partner.*

An Executive who is feeling stuck with their Executive Assistant's plate of responsibilities and cannot seem to find it within themselves to delegate more or deeper into their task list might be frozen themselves. They need to evaluate it from an inward perspective first before they can attempt to solve that problem externally. If I sit down on a given day and I have 200% more workload than I can get done in a given day, I have no option but to delegate. I believe what happens is that some leaders don't have more than they can handle on their plate because they haven't challenged themselves. You have to own that if you think I may be writing to you. As an Executive, if you do not have the ability or the burning desire to delegate more, I contend that you may not be adequately challenging yourself.

What is the long-term time-savings cost?

JOAN: *This is probably the most important question to ask yourself. "How much time will you save long term?" The example I have is if it takes you two hours to teach your EA how to do a monthly report that will save you 2 hours, over a year you will save a valuable 24 hours. This is an investment in future savings and productivity, and you will also create margin and time to work on other priorities you have but can never seem to get to. I suggest taking two hours to teach the EA how to do the report, including where to get the numbers and what report format to use to display the information. As an EA, I saved my Executive 24 hours annually by preparing a report every month for him.*

What can your Executive Assistant do for you?

JOAN: *Some tasks your EA could potentially assume for you might include:*

- *Compile your direct reports' work summaries for the weekly report to management, including making the inevitable follow ups to tardy folks?*

- *Track your organization's quarterly required compliance training and follow up on your behalf to ensure your team reaches 100% training compliance?*

- *Track monthly expenses in a spreadsheet to help forecast the following fiscal year budget?*

What could you be spending your time on that has bigger impact than what you could delegate to your strategic partner?

JAMES: *Some investments are simple and grow along a flat line. Investment is where I put an hour into something or a dollar into something and I get a dollar or an hour back with earned interest. But the relationship and the investment should be looked at from a compounding interest perspective, which means today I invested 2 hours and I got a net impact of 12-hour savings.*

I invested 2 hours to save 12 hours which saves 24 hours or 36 hours or 40 hours because it allows me to work on these other high value things. So, instead of a flat interest line, you get a compounding interest kind of investment. Investment is the perfect word to use for the training and development of an Executive Assistant and Executive relationship.

It is important to ask yourself, "How can I work at the top of my licensure?" I like to use the analogy of a doctor's office because doctors in the medical profession have really done a good job of working at the top of licensure. When you walk into the doctor's office, whose job is it to greet you? Not your doctor. They have someone who greets and checks you in.

Then someone else brings you to the examination room, still not the doctor. That person's job is to make sure you are who you say you are, get your weight, check your temperature, and find out what the purpose of the visit is. Then perhaps you need blood work, and they bring in another person that is highly trained in drawing blood (still not the doctor). This person is more trained than the previous one. In some doctor's offices, the attending professional may still not even be the doctor; a physician's assistant starts the examination, reviews your medical history, and makes some of their own notes. It is not until the very end that the doctor comes in, reviews everything and gives you 3 minutes of time to answer any of your serious questions and then signs off on the course of action. This is an extremely efficient example of top of licensure in work. If every Executive could learn from a doctor's office, they could introduce a similar effectiveness and impact.

JOAN: *I love to talk about this because most people, not just Executives, will think "This only takes me a few minutes. It is no big deal to answer an email or schedule a meeting." Well, how many times a day or week are you doing that? Minutes add up to hours and weeks.*

5 hours/week x 52 weeks/year =
250+ hours working on things an EA can manage.

Are you really bringing the best value to your organization when you do those things?

JAMES: *Two thoughts come to mind as you talk about that:*
- *The first thought is around focus. It is an important component of the decision to delegate. Can I give it the attention it needs or is my EA more equipped to focus on the issue at hand with a little guidance from me?*

- *The second is an extension of the doctor analogy. If a doctor spends 2 hours with every patient in a 10-hour workday, they get to see five patients. If the doctor can spend 20 minutes with each patient (which is a long time in today's medical world), they can see as many as 30 patients in a day, effectively multiplying their impact by SIX TIMES. Six times the impact on people's lives, six times the help in society, and six times the revenue.*

JOAN: *The following two article excerpts will hopefully provide context about the dangers of multitasking and its downsides:*

The Cost of Multitasking: How Much Productivity Is Lost Through Task Switching?
(Source: Wrike®, a Citrix Company)

Oftentimes, multi-tasking has the effect of making people think they are accomplishing more. The truth is that multi-tasking and task switching can have detrimental effects on productivity.

When we jump from task to task, we are not really getting more done. In actuality, we're forcing our brains to constantly switch gears, working harder to do things at a lower level of quality and exhausting our mental reserves.

We multitask in many ways, but regardless of the form, the cost of context switching and task switching is high. It is unrealistic for most of us to eradicate the multitasking and task switching monsters altogether. But with a better understanding of how it impacts our productivity (and which personality types are most vulnerable), we can reduce context switching productivity loss.

But Multi-Tasking Is Productive ... Right?
(Source: Psychology Today)

Does this describe you? While you are on a teleconference call you are writing up your quarterly report, checking your email, and texting your friend about where you are meeting for lunch. You would say that you are good at multi-tasking, right? You might want to re-think your strategy. Recent estimates are that you can lose up to 40% of your productivity if you multi-task.

The term "multi-tasking" is actually a misnomer. People cannot actually do more than one task at a time. Instead, we switch tasks. The term that is used in the research is "task switching."

Task switching is "expensive." There has been a lot of research on task switching, but the common thread is you can only do so much at one time with your brain. By not having enough mental margin, you exhaust yourself and degrade productivity, not increase it. When we do too much at once, or switch tasks in seconds, we become mentally frayed at the edges. Our emotions run short, we lose ability to concentrate, and our stress levels soar.

> "Why is my role always seen as a supplemental want rather than a strategic need?"
>
> **—Anonymous**
> *Executive Assistant*

What is your Executive Assistant's willingness and eagerness to take on new responsibilities?

JOAN: *When I worked as an EA, I was always willing and eager to take on MORE. I wanted to grow my skill set, learn new things, understand my Executive's world, and increase my responsibilities. Many of the younger EAs today are eager to dig in and be their Executive's partner. Many seasoned EAs are more than eager to be a partner and have learned how to do so. My advice is to pay attention, be aware, pick up on verbal and written cues from your EA, and be a good listener. Ask, "How would you like to expand your job/role? What skills do you have that I am not utilizing? What types of responsibilities would you like to take on?"*

What areas of responsibility do I currently have that I would most like to see my EA handle?

JOAN: *As a busy Executive it would be very difficult and time-consuming to type, dictate, or write my list of what I do every day or weekly or quarterly.*

I apply a philosophy I have successfully used for years: look at incoming work with a question mark, not a period. Period means the end, this is it, and there is no better. No one else can do this as well as me. If I have a question mark in my head as I go through my day, I will ask myself questions like:

- *Can I give this to my EA to manage?*
- *What if I teach my EA to write this contract? Imagine how much time that would save me with future contracts!*
- *Could my EA have handled that call?*
- *Could my EA have delegated this task to someone on my behalf?*
- *Could my EA streamline this process?*
- *What if my EA managed this project?*
- *What aspects of this project could my EA manage?*
- *What could my EA do to start this project for me?*

Who knows better about what they can help you with than the Executive Assistant? What is the Executive doing every day that the EA looks at and thinks, "Why is my leader not delegating that to me? I did that for five years for another Executive. I am highly qualified in my role and have the skill set to accomplish it 10 times faster."

A Brief Checklist of Delegation Ideas

JOAN: *I want you to start thinking about what you could delegate to your EA that encompasses both basic and more complex work.*

There are so many ways an Executive Assistant can add greater value to a task, project, or initiative. And the EA can move out into fresh areas and grow their skills. Here are some examples:

- **Analysis**
  - *Create presentations*
  - *Analyze trends in office technology*
  - *Attention to details*
  - *Develop spreadsheets*
  - *Compilation and distribution of reports*
- **Business Competencies**
  - *Not overwhelmed by or addicted to technology*
  - *Track completion of follow-up tasks*
  - *Discuss problems and solutions with Executive*
  - *Demonstrate mindfulness and being "present"*
  - *Demonstrate an interest in ongoing learning and development*
  - *Organize tasks, projects, and other assignments*
  - *Promote positive image of the office*
  - *Keen sense of what is urgent and what can wait*
  - *Display mastery of skills (in planning meetings, maintaining action logs, maintaining the Executive's schedule, coordinating executive reports, and more)*
- **Communication**
  - *Represent the Executive in business meetings*
  - *Delegate and explain tasks to other support staff*
  - *Write courtesy notes and cards on behalf of Executive*
  - *Make calls on behalf of Executive*
  - *Monitor and manage Executive's emails*
  - *Draft and edit correspondence on Executive's behalf*
  - *Handle telephone calls on behalf of the Executive*
  - *Stay connected with clients and stakeholders via social media.*
  - *Manage social networking for the leader, organization, or company*

- **Coordination**
  - *Organize and coordinate multiple projects*
  - *Coordinate accomplishment of the Executive's priority tasks.*
  - *Coordinate on-site meetings*
  - *Coordinate off-site meetings including preview, select, and contract venues*
- **Executive Support**
  - *Ensure that the Executive is organized, on time, and well prepared for whatever lies ahead*
  - *Help ensure that the Executive is compliant for required training for business conduct, data privacy, and anti-harassment, etc.*
  - *Find training opportunities that fit Executive's schedule for maintaining professional license requirements*
  - *Promote a balanced life for the Executive*
  - *Demonstrate the capacity to provide comprehensive professional and personal support*
  - *Manage Executive's brand*
- **Ethical Behaviors**
  - *Keep confidential information confidential*
  - *Protect the integrity and confidentiality of Executive's position*
  - *Advise the Executive concerning ethical factors*
- **Financial**
  - *Manage budget, bills, and invoices*
  - *Track and process renewals for periodicals, subscriptions, associations, and memberships*
- **Liaison.**
  - *Outstanding liaison with external contacts and business colleagues*
  - *Act as a liaison for other leaders or key people*

- **Mentoring/Leadership**
  - *Resolve conflicts in the office*
  - *Counsel administrative staff about performance*
- **Office Operations**
  - *Obtain backups of Executive's tech, such as chargers, cords, and peripheral accessories*
  - *Operate and troubleshoot office equipment*
  - *Assist with organizational outsourcing*
- **Procedures**
  - *Recommend improved systems and procedures for daily operations*
  - *Streamline office procedures*
  - *Recommend improved systems and procedures*
- **Research**
  - *Gather background information and materials for meetings*
  - *Collect statistics to substantiate information or to verify findings*
  - *Input and maintain information on project tracking tool*
  - *Provide cost and features information for future purchases*
  - *Compile site information for cities and venues meeting criteria for offsite retreats*
  - *Assess current workplace trends and how it affects the business*
- **Strategy**
  - *Manage the Executive's calendar from a strategic perspective*
- **Travel**
  - *Prepare travel itineraries, contact list, meeting materials; process visa application, arrange travel immunization appointment*
  - *Help visitors with travel and on-site arrangements for their visit*

Discuss Task Expectations

What if you think your EA should take something on but they do not agree? Or vice versa? You need to have a conversation. You each must explain your reasoning. The other party may counter that reasoning. If so, you both need to discuss it and come to an agreement. Be sure to listen to why your EA does not want to take on an assignment. Maybe they don't feel skilled in that area, or they are not the most qualified person to take it on. Or maybe your EA is quite capable of handling the task and you just hadn't thought of it.

Release Slowly

We slowly release and delegate. We do not dump everything at once. You delegate a few tasks and observe the feedback loop. You should not assume that your EA will get something new right the first time, nor should you assume, they will get it wrong. You may have to be patient for the feedback, but once you have it, you will know what to do next. As you see your EA can effectively handle matters and make sound judgment calls, then release more.

JAMES: *I utilize two phases of the Executive/Executive Assistant relationship: Tactical and Strategic.*

Phase I: Tactical Executive/EA Relationship

Phase I is more tactical, so when preparing an initial list, ask yourself as an Executive what you would like to assign. Share the list with your Executive Assistant and then openly ask for feedback and input as to what tactical assignments can be listed that would help reach the strategic objectives and goals.

Example #1: *If the strategic objectives and goals of an Executive are to raise revenue, reduce expenses, interface with the employees more, and spend more time with the clients, then what tactical assignments can be* *made to ensure that those things happen or to assist to ensure those things happen? To increase revenue, the Executive needs to sell more. The Executive Assistant can find opportunities, calendar those opportunities, and help to get the Executive in the rooms where decisions are made.*

Example #2: *If the strategic objective is to interface with the employees more from a team building exercise perspective, what tactical things can the Executive Assistant do? They can schedule time with the Executive and the employees. They can write scripts for the Executive to memorize and use in those interfaces. They can create opportunities for virtual town halls or in-person town halls. They can handle all of the tactical components needed, such as booking the room, setting up the technology to be used, putting the employees in the room at the same time as the Executive.*

As we migrate into Phase II, these assignments will have to become strategic as well.

What strategic initiatives and assignments can be made to further develop the strategic objectives? When you get to that phase, and I think that goes back to your comment about when the Executive feels like they have assigned as much as they can, I think this is where they could become frozen when it is time to engage the Executive Assistant on strategy—into the strategic mapping. That is when the Executive Assistant becomes a strategic partner.

JOAN: *In my book, Become an Inner Circle Assistant, I talk about the EA as a cognitive being, not just an order taker and task doer. Cognitive being EAs engage all their senses at work. They use their brains. They are not working on autopilot. They operate at a much higher level. This would tie into the Phase I Tactical Executive/EA Relationship that James is writing about in this section.*

Phase II: Strategic Executive/EA Relationship

JAMES: *It is all a kind of cognitive thought hierarchy pyramid. At the foundation of the cognitive hierarchy are the individuals that are thinking one or two steps into a task. However, as you travel up that hierarchical pyramid, the tactical partnership becomes more strategic, and the individual can see many steps into the initiative and can map alternative routes to achieve success. Developed trust must be foundational to satisfy tactical plans and initiatives as the partnership starts to migrate towards the top of that pyramid. Once you and your EA reach the top third of the pyramid, you are in the strategic partnership range. Your EA must be able to think strategically most of the time. They did not just come into their role that way. You developed together to become strategic partners; they have to understand the strategy to become a strategic partner. They must understand the types of strategic initiatives the Executive prefers. The EA has to start to think like the Executive. They do not necessarily have to be the Executive or be just like the Executive, but they have to think like them. If the Executive Assistant becomes a cognitive extension of the Executive, they have hit the pinnacle of that pyramid. That pinnacle of the cognitive hierarchy is when you become one mind in your actions.*

JOAN: *Here is a brief list of what strategic EAs do:*

- *Engage in the scope of business direction and goals.*
- *Perform supervisory responsibilities—interview, hire, mentor, and train other EAs or interns.*
- *Work directly with C-level and senior management team members.*
- *Coordinate Earnings Call logistics, post-earnings callbacks to analysts and investor marketing road shows.*
- *Assist senior management on confidential mergers and acquisitions.*
- *Work with governmental relations, legislative and political communities.*

- *Perform special projects and research.*
- *Balance priorities and adapt to various changing environments, projects, and personnel.*
- *Work in a constantly changing environment and streamline a hectic day.*
- *Be a hands-on problem solver and task driver.*
- *Ensure adherence to corporate policies.*
- *Plan special events.*
- *Build relationships with stakeholders, Executive management team, and clients.*
- *Operate as a resourceful team player.*
- *Achieve high performance goals.*
- *Communicate creatively.*
- *Engage in forward thinking.*
- *Ensure Executive's brand is consistently communicated.*
- *Provide sophisticated calendar management, prioritizing inquiries and requests while troubleshooting conflicts.*
- *Design and produce complex documents, reports, and presentations.*
- *Provide Personal Assistant support, including supervising Executive's wealth management team, personal banking, and coordinating family matters.*
- *Orchestrate offsite Executive and client meetings and retreats.*

JAMES: *One challenge I think Executive Assistants may encounter is when they hit the point in time when they are masterful in the tactical phase but haven't yet been invited into the strategic space. There is a layer of frustration. I have read in Joan's books various points relating to how the Executive and EA have got to work at that Stage 3 strategic relationship to allow everybody to move into the strategic space together.*

Let us talk about this explicitly. So, what happens, in my opinion, is that you are building this trust over time. It is this evolving relationship and eventually there is this line where the Executive has to invite you in. They have to invite you into that room. Bringing you into that room is a risk for that Executive. Remember that responsibility conversation? At the end of the day the Executive is still the responsible party, even if they delegated the activity to their EA. One of the risks is that if I invite that Executive Assistant into the space and they cannot handle the strategy—they cannot cognitively connect beyond that tactical layer—then one of two things is likely to happen, or possibly both:

- *The relationship between the Executive and the Executive Assistant will feel strange. It will be stressed because it is a new initial point in which the Executive Assistant has to prove themself again. Although they proved themself in the tactical space, now they have to start all over in a new proving ground on the strategic component. If this happens, it will likely be a long haul, but it is possible to overcome.*

- *The Executive will retreat from the relationship and revert to tackling the initiatives themselves. If this happens, it is difficult to repair the relationship.*

The line between the tactical and strategic zones is not a bold line. It is a fuzzy space where you can migrate in and out of it, sometimes without even recognizing that you are strategically thinking and interacting. You can evolve through the space together and it is less contentious because it is just happening organically. But if I, as an Executive, say to my EA, "You've been my EA. You have done a great job on these tactical things. Now I would like you to join me strategically." What am I doing? I am testing them again. I am watching for it, and I am testing. If they have not been trained up or haven't been in that role before, they're probably going to fail on some things. That's okay, if I understand it is going to happen and the Executive/EA relationship is such that there is room for that.

JOAN: *This is only if an EA wants that. Some EAs are very content, so they do not care, and they will never be strategic partners. And that is okay, too, as we need those types of people in the company as well. We went through a period of time when I had my EA strategic partner and an Administrative Assistant who managed basic duties, the office, ordering supplies, and organizing training aids and props, etc. We wanted to move the Administrative Assistant to an Executive Assistant position to support me and my EA strategic partner, but the Administrative Assistant did not want that. She needed to maintain certain hours because of children at home and probably did not want the extra pressure. That was fine, as we still had a need for what that role was and continued to be.*

JAMES: *I absolutely understand that, just like some Executives will never become CEO or make Partner. With those EAs who are clearly not willing or able to be strategic partners, what will likely happen is that the risk of initiative failure is too substantial, so the Executives are apprehensive to invite the EA in. Those EAs will recognize that and accept it.*

A challenging situation is that an EA may want the strategic partnership, but the Executive may recognize that they are not ready or that the required foundational trust is not adequate. What I have seen happen is that if you do not invite the Executive Assistant into that figurative strategic room, resentment grows. The moment resentment starts, the mind starts going into some peculiar thoughts such as, "Does the Executive think I do not belong in that room? Does the Executive not believe in me and my abilities to satisfy those higher-level organizational demands? Am I not good enough?" As soon as some of those thoughts get layered into the relationship, you have got some work to do if you intend on ever getting to a strategic partnership.

JOAN: *I like the word organic. When I look at the EAs I have had who grew into partnership with me (not all of them did), it happened organically. We started their jobs with the fundamentals. Then I started handing off other tasks to them. As I saw them become confident in those tasks and I was pleased with their work, I delegated more challenging, robust assignments and projects.*

For the Naysayer Executive

JOAN: *There are Executives who will say, "I will never do that. This person is here to just do the tactical." That is okay, but **do not expect the same amazing results** as if you put work into building a strategic partnership.*

The Value of Human Moments

Communicating regularly with your Executive Assistant may sound like a no-brainer, but how and how often you communicate with your strategic partner makes all the difference and will provide you and your business with a Competitive Edge.

JOAN: *I coined the term "human moments" 30 years ago. Put simply, human moments are when we are sitting face-to-face with others. No technology is involved. In 2020, when the pandemic hit, people could no longer have human moments. We were told to stay as far away from others as we could. This really broke a lot of personal relations, disrupted business, and created havoc. Eventually society got comfortable and accepted that way of living and working.*

As things began opening up again, the business world began to move to hybrid office environments. Some organizations stayed completely with the WFH (work from home) model, and other companies wanted their employees back in the office, although this was delayed numerous times because of COVID variants surging regionally or nationally.

Without realizing it, employees and leaders were becoming disconnected. Yes, they said they were more productive than ever. But what about the HUMAN relationship? It suffered. Employees said they did not feel connected to their corporate culture. They missed spontaneous brainstorming in the hallway or synergistic conference room sessions. They felt isolated. This cannot be good for society or business. There were significant increases in mental health issues and crises across the board: children, teenagers, AND adults. Seemingly overnight we were all talking about these mental health issues and many companies actively addressed these areas with tools, counseling benefits, and just acknowledgement that mental health was severely compromised.

Many EAs felt their Executive forgot about them and did not even touch base with them weekly. Yet other EAs were highly in demand and their Executives relied on them to keep the ship afloat.
More than ever, our society needs human moments. The number of

people suffering with anxiety, depression, frustration, and anger has significantly risen. There has been an increase in suicide rates and drug overdoses. I am certain this is due to not having human interaction. As a society, the majority of people think they are interacting with others because they are on Facebook, LinkedIn, or Twitter, or texting and IM'ing all the time. That is NOT human interaction. I am concerned about the younger generation who do not have:

- *Social skills.*
- *The courage to have uncomfortable conversations.*
- *Ability to deal with difficult people so they hide behind technology.*
- *Writing and tactful communication skills.*
- *High self-esteem because everyone else portrays they have a fantastic life.*
- *Meaningful relationships.*
- *Coping skills to deal with stress.*
- *Patience (want instant gratification).*
- *A feeling of fulfillment.*

And these are the people who are going to be leading your businesses in the future! I strongly believe that as leaders, we need to appropriately lead people—we need to set the bar high—and it starts with your EA. The two of you should be an example to the others in your department, division, or company. I always say, "It takes courage to not follow the crowd. The crowd may be going in the wrong direction."

JAMES: *As the Executive, it is true you do not want to spend time having to go through the details with your EA and the EA usually wants more detail. I struggle with this because it usually means I have to slow down, at first. It is painful. I must have clear intent to slow down in order take the time to provide that level of information to my EA. What I have learned and continue to learn, is that the more I slow down and provide greater detail up front, the less often my EA will need to ask me* to do that. For example, my EA has learned I do not want to slow down, so if she sees me trying to give details to her, she takes it and runs with it and recognizes I am trying. My EA will ask, "What do you want me to do with this?" and will even push back on me a little bit. Then, she will encourage me to go fast again and will do whatever she can to help me run fast.

The most important details are used by your EA to clarify the context around something you have asked them to accomplish. As your EA, the context around your purpose and your mission is critical so they can do a better job at determining the best, most efficient path forward. Give your EA context around what you are saying. For example, with a meeting, what is your vision or your goal for that meeting? With context for the meeting, your EA can determine the menu, the length, their own role during the meeting, the agenda, etc. without any additional details from you, thus speeding you up in the long run!

JOAN: Let us talk about travel. Executives tell me they want their EA to walk their entire trip in their head from the time the Executive departs the house until arriving back home. And to map out the trip in a way that makes sense.

JAMES: That totally makes sense however, for a strategic partner EA, it is much more than that. One of the mechanisms that I use to satisfy an EA's need for information is to provide the top three most important goals for a trip.

For example, here are the three things I have to accomplish:
- Mergers and acquisitions trip - I need to seal this deal.
- Meet with a really important client.
- Go to the gym with this long-time friend from my college days.

This context functionally anchors the primary objectives of the trip. The only way to get that clarity is some form of direct communication. I have to either say out loud that these are the three most important things, or this is the goal of the trip. Obviously with back story and enough vision laid out ahead of time, an Executive Assistant and Executive should be able to get there together. The EA should be looking at all those pieces and strategically thinking about what makes sense and do the critical thinking. Then, the EA may be able to work in secondary or tertiary objectives to maximize the value of the trip, only after satisfying the stated intent and primary objectives.

JOAN: *As an Executive, I love what you are saying about direct communication. It gives me a chance to clarify expectations and perceptions with my EA. We cannot clarify things so well in text messages and emails. I do not want to go back and forth 20 times detail by detail. If we talk for five minutes, we get things clarified. A lot of times as I am talking through something with Melia, I'm thinking, "Oh, yeah, I thought about this, and that reminds me I have got to do that."*

JAMES: *Joan, how do you view some of the tools that have been created over the past 20 years that are virtual huddle tools? And how has that changed the relationship between the Executive and their EA?*

JOAN: *I feel good about the tools that have been developed. They should be leveraged in conjunction with having the human connection. I have a daily morning huddle with my EA because we must keep information flowing in our fast-paced world. I am a big fan of an in-person, or at least a live on-screen virtual, morning huddle. I believe this prevents a frequent problem EAs face when such conversations do not occur.*

Huge Void for Executive Assistants

JOAN: *The EA has to keep information and projects moving. The challenge today is there is this huge void for these struggling EAs working with Executives who want to "do their own thing." The EA is not invited into the conversation or copied on emails. If I am your EA and I am not in the loop, I cannot:*

- *Be the best partner for you.*
- *Anticipate problems.*
- *Prevent fires from happening.*
- *Eliminate non-essential emails and other communications.*
- *Determine who to let through to you or not.*
- *Forecast your calendar for months in advance.*
- *Understand your sense of urgency.*
- *Take the lead on an action.*

JAMES: *Nowadays, people can go around the EA a lot more efficiently. For me, having to circle back around to ensure the information that has gone around my EA reaches my EA is more work. It is not more efficient for me. Commitment has to be made to recognize that ultimately, although it was more work upfront to get that information to your EA or your strategic partner, it was less work in the long run.*

That is what is hard for young Executives who are fast paced, tech-forward, and a less structured Executive. I am putting myself in a lot of those buckets because I can get a text message or a WhatsApp message or a short quick audio clip on my phone. I can respond to it and the decision is done and it moves on. If I do not stop and realize that from that communication, there could be 20 more communications down the line, like a string of emails, and if I do not tag my EA, I have to respond to every one of those future communications. If I tag my EA in early enough and do the work up front to get that information flowing through her instead of me, then it saves me in the long run. I think that is really hard for Executives to recognize because it is somewhat counterintuitive without experience.

Here is an example: I have these guys in construction that I have worked with for many years. I came up through the business with them, way before becoming the CEO of the organization. I started out as an intern while working with some of these guys. As I got into project and people management, these clients could call me and or text me at any time, 24 hours a day, 7 days a week, because it is early hours for construction guys who may contact me to say, "Hey, can you come out and look at this concrete slab we just poured?" I had to run out to the job site, check it out, and go on to the next task. I do not have the flexibility in my schedule to do that as often as I used to be able to and more importantly, if I go out to the site alone, I miss a huge opportunity to tag in one of my team members at work to lead the interaction. If I get that text message now, I am more likely to text back and tell them that I am really busy today, but I can come out tomorrow. That is all well and good since I scheduled it and can make it happen, but guess who they are going to text next time, and the next time, and the next time? It is me, and I am not the best person to coordinate with to get the best service from our firm!

If I had tagged my strategic partner in at that point, and written something like, "I really appreciate our relationship and am grateful that you reached out to me directly. Just so you know, I have taken on some new responsibilities in the office, and I have a much more difficult schedule to monitor in order to get me to the site. Can you work with my EA who is CC'ed on this text to set up a time for us to meet? She will also ensure I have one of my technical leaders from the office with me when we meet so you get the chance to connect with the brilliant person doing the work behind the scenes."

Every client that I have done this with understands, is receptive and "gets it." I have actually strengthened my relationships with clients through this methodology because I have become more accountable and dependable. My EA is just going to make sure that it happens. Because I have tagged her in from the beginning of that conversation, it saves me so much work downstream.

It Is a Matter of Commitment

JOAN: *I often hear Executives say, "I do not have time to talk to my Executive Assistant in the morning. I hit the ground running." I understand. My work brain starts at 5:30 a.m. and I am in high gear when I see my EA at 8:00 a.m.*

But the truth is, I do not buy this. As I told you, I worked as an Executive Assistant for a Vice President who worked very long days, weekends, and traveled extensively, who attended back-to-back meetings. Yet he still made time for me. Another example of commitment is many Executives hit the gym at 5:00 a.m. Obviously, it is important enough to them that they get up early to dress and drive to the gym. Things that are absolutely important to us, we will make time for, unless there is a life crisis.

I often hear Executive Assistants say, "I cannot bother my Executive. They are too busy." Or "I can't ask my Executive to have a morning talk with me."

But the truth is, when an EA says this to me, I see a lack of respect for themselves. They are basically saying they don't "deserve" your time. They obviously do not see themselves as a partner because you would certainly take time at 7:30 or 8:00 a.m. to talk to a direct report.

JOAN: *Going back to the football analogy I stated earlier. The players huddle before running a play. So that is all you are doing with your EA. Having a quick huddle to confirm the day's play or to strategize. And some days, you may not huddle.*

Benefits of One-on-One Meetings

JOAN: *As you know, I have worked on both sides of the desk for many years, 20 as an EA, and 32+ as an Executive. There are numerous benefits to you and your EA when you make time to have one-on-ones or huddles, whatever you want to call them.*

As mentioned, I have coached 300+ Executives. At every one of those coaching sessions, I recommended the Executive implement this practice. If they already were having daily huddles, we discussed how they could make those meetings even better. The feedback from the Executives is always the same: "Joan, this is the best thing you taught me and the one thing that has had the greatest impact on our relationship and productivity."

What are the benefits of morning huddles?
- Reduces stress.
- Diminishes last-minute chaos.
- Opens lines of communication.
- Clarifies expectations for both parties.
- Both parties understand the day's priorities.
- Flags issues or situations that might arise.
- Makes working together more enjoyable.
- Provides the Executive with status updates.

- Helps the Executive get organized for the day.
- Right hand knows what the left hand is doing.
- EA will more effectively complete work assignments.

The #1 Best Piece of Advice

JOAN: *In coaching 300+ executives over 30+ years on how to work with their EA, the #1 piece of advice they told me that made the biggest difference in their relationship and productivity was the daily huddle. Need I say more?*

P.S. An EA is going to "huddle" with the Executive they support the most. It is not reasonable to expect an EA to have daily huddles with everyone they support.

What Would You Two Discuss?

If you are wondering what to discuss in a huddle with your EA, here are a few ideas:

Daily Calendars

Technology is not perfect, and neither are humans. It is easy to place a wrong time or wrong date on a calendar. Or because so many Executives are independent, they place events on their own calendars and forget to inform their Executive Assistant partner.

Accuracy in scheduling is extremely important. Executives are too busy to have hiccups in their schedules. Plus, it is embarrassing to the Executive or the EA who set the schedule.

It is always best to review the day's events together. Many EAs are doing research, preparing outgoing pre-reads, and filtering email note strings for their Executive in preparation for a meeting.

This is also the time to discuss any meetings or travel that was scheduled or assigned since yesterday.

Discuss Email Communications

When it comes to email management, there are various approaches. Some Executives want their EA to read all their emails and act on those emails. Another approach is the Executive who wants to manage all their own emails and then forward specific emails to their EA as appropriate.

Your daily huddles are to update each other on email communications, whether it is a status update or clarifying new actions to be taken.

Visitors

Discuss any events that external visitors will attend and anticipate actions to be taken before and during their visit.

Department Issues

This is a good time to discuss any departmental problems that need attention. EAs are often privy to information within the department or are aware of potential personnel issues.

Status Updates

The EA can update you, the Executive, with updates on projects, meetings, items they are working on, and any other pertinent information. Ask your EA to begin providing these updates in your daily huddles if they are not already doing so. Executives do not like to have to ask for the status of projects and tasks. (Nor do they have the time.)

Upcoming Travel

Traveling is quite complex, especially since 2020. It will save a tremendous amount of time and energy if you and your EA discuss anticipated trips and trips that need to be scheduled.

Follow-Up Items

Whether you and your EA use an app or software program to track action items and follow up, it is also good to discuss these with each other.

Training and Development

Development happens when we take conscious action to improve. It is not a "check the box" aspect of a career. Be sure to make time to discuss your EA's requirements for professional development. What tools does your EA need to have that will streamline their work?

Special Projects

What special projects are you working on or are coming up in the next few weeks? Is there any research that needs to be done? Will information necessary for the project be coming from others inside or outside of the company? Are presentations, graphs or charts required?

Time: Investment or Expense?

It might initially appear as though these meetings might involve a tremendous amount of time, but they do not when you meet on a regular basis because things do not have a chance to build up or back up. In fact, it keeps everything flowing smoothly, reduces chances of missed details or tasks falling through the cracks, eliminates chaos, and reduces last-minute time crunches. Whether you view time spent as an investment or an expense can often be based on the filter with which you view time in general.

Getting Started

Changing behaviors and habits that have been with us for a long time is never easy. You may notice that after you have tried to have daily huddles for a few days that you want to stop. The reason this usually occurs is because it is uncomfortable.

JOAN: *I want to encourage you to stay with the process. At least try it for 30 days. I have heard Executives say they miss these daily huddles with their Executive Assistant once they engage in the process and miss a day or few days. They realize these communication opportunities are critical.*

Follow these helpful tips to get started:

1. *Start by meeting one morning a week. You might start with Monday or Friday to discuss the upcoming week.*

2. *Gradually increase meetings to two days, and then three days, and so on. Your goal is to have a daily huddle with each other whether in-person, virtually, or by telephone. Of course, sometimes this is just not possible.*

3. *When you meet on a regular basis, the huddles will not consume a great deal of time because you keep the communication about items/information moving between you. Meetings will take more time when the EA or Executive have been out of the office for several days. But you and your EA can easily catch up!*

Putting It All Together: The Maximized Executive Assistant

Now that we have discussed the art of delegation and the value of daily huddles, we will discuss how to maximize the value your Executive Assistant can bring to you and your organization.

A Word About Busy Work vs. Value Work

When we talk about delegating more work to your EA, we are not necessarily saying more busy work. You want to assign or transfer tasks of higher value to your EA, otherwise they are just a "task doer" and not a strategic partner.

When You Delegate

Some things to consider as you begin to delegate to your Executive Assistant are:

- ***Explain the WHY, not just the how.*** *When you explain the "why" of something, your EA will be better able to figure it out when approached with a similar situation in the future.*

JOAN: *A great example in my business are client contracts. I wrote all the client contracts until my EA learned the "what, why, and how" of reviewing a contract. I also am presented with complex, lengthy contracts from government agencies or large corporations. I must read every line in that contract. I may have questions or not agree with something, or we need to add an addendum. When I teach my EA how to handle that type of contract, I explain why I am questioning something or what my EA needs to ensure we do on our end. For example, a client may have specific invoicing requirements; some clients do not permit us to use their company logo in advertising; these items need to be clearly highlighted in their contract so we can abide by the terms and conditions of the contract. This is important business.*

- **Provide the big picture.** If we are working on a new course with several modules, various format offerings, and several touch points, I first explain the big picture of the project and the expected outcome. Then I dive back into the details or the aspects of what my EA must handle or delegate to other staff. The benefits of this are my EA:
  - Might see a missing piece of the puzzle.
  - Sees how the pieces of the puzzle must fit together.
  - Can anticipate work and be proactive.
  - Knows who the players are ahead of time.

- **Take time to hand it over properly.** This will save time and potential errors in the future. We have to make time to save time. When we rush to turn over a task, we leave out little pieces that could ultimately:
  - Cause our Executive Assistant to go down the wrong path with the project.
  - Slow the EA down in the ability to move forward.
  - Create confusion and chaos.
  - Lead to embarrassment for you or your EA.

Verbalizing Constructive Observations

JOAN: As you delegate tasks and assignments to your EA, you should give on-the-spot feedback as to whether the work returned to you met your expectations and looked like you anticipated it would. For example, every year we launch several new classes, books, or events. We have to track every aspect of each project by using a customized tracker for each project. In the tracker we identify who is overseeing what part of the projects, project milestone dates, costs involved, review dates, and completion dates. In my mind, I have an idea of how I want the project tracker to *look so it is easy for me to use and intuitive with how I process information. I also know how sections of a new project or course need to be broken out. When my EA first works on that project tracker, she may not exactly know what I am thinking or what I expect it to look like. My EA does her best, but it may not exactly match what I see in my head. So, I need to let my EA know where she missed the target, what to change or what is missing. Once my EA knows that she applies those design elements and expectations to similar projects.*

Even after Executives and EAs have worked together for years, an Executive still needs to provide feedback about what they like, their expectations, what their EA can do better, or what their EA can stop doing. Do not assume things stay the same because our lives and work do not stay the same. Plus, we are always being exposed to new, better, faster ways of doing our work.

Executives are not always eager to provide this input. When I ask Executives why they do not have open and respectful conversations about these things with their EA, they tell me:

- *"I am not sure how my EA will respond."*
- *"What if my EA gets emotional or defensive?"*
- *"I assume my EA knows what needs to be done."*
- *"My EA should know my preferences."*

Well, they do not. Executive Assistants are not mind readers! Your EA cannot meet your expectations or get onto the same page with you, if you do not let them know what you are thinking. My rule of thumb is to tell my EA what I like about what she has done so she continues to do that. Then I will specifically point out what needs to be changed, adjusted, or deleted.

Stop, Start, More Please!

JOAN: *You also should be open to your EA giving you feedback. Remember, you are a team; you are working in partnership. In one of my workshops for assistants, early in the class I ask the attendees, "Tell me one thing you would like your Executive to either stop doing, start doing, or do more often?" They always have answers for me. Then I coach them on how to approach their Executive to talk about it.*

You can easily ask your EA this question. You can discuss this monthly, or quarterly, or even in a daily huddle.

Executive Assistant Talent: Tech Leader

JAMES: *I am generally considered to be a younger Executive, but I would have to say that I am not super techie. I am not the person that, for my age (37), is going to rely on technology for the day-to-day jobs. But there are pieces of the technological tools that we have available to us that we can rely on to make us better at our jobs; make us more effective in our positions. I have used a number of different tools, from work traits profile software, dashboarding for KPIs, project management tools, and finance software.*

I find that the tools that I like the most are the ones that are based on sharing information in a nonverbal or verbal way between the two parties improving the communication effectiveness because that is probably the hardest thing to maintain when you're traveling across the country in and out of airplanes. I move fast so if I do not have a way to effectively communicate or a set of tools to help me with that, it is much harder to maintain that relationship.

JOAN: *One thing I always say is that you can have the greatest tool or app in the world, but it is not the end all and be all. It is your thinking behind the tool. An Executive Assistant (or the Executive) might have a great project tracker but does not know how to strategically map the timeline; or cannot think about it logically; or is not creative so they do not use color coding to save time. Or it is a platform for capturing to-do items and tracking follow-up and completion. But if the EA forgets to enter the updates in the tracker, then it is of no use. Maybe the EA is such a concise writer they do not provide enough detail about the progress of the project. I am not making this stuff up—I have seen it happen.*

JAMES: *If the goal is to use technology to replace the communication altogether, you are heading in the wrong direction—it should be to enhance the communication. Traditionally Kayla and I use tech tools to either create agendas, to enhance the conversations when we do meet for our one-on-ones, or to increase the speed of communication. The world is moving much faster than it used to and that is not going to change. The speed of communication must increase the speed of trust. We have to use those tools to enhance that.*

These tools can become like a dark hole for Executives as they think to themselves, "I have to communicate with all these other people. I do not want to slow down and spend this time with my EA." They have gotten it all wrong. They need to look at these tools and say this is intended to make me more effective because a lot of times the Executive is the one who is the poor communicator. For example, a lot of times I am moving too fast. I do not provide enough clarity. I do not give details. But the tool can create a platform for my EA to say, "Could you slow down? Could you give me some more detail?" And that helps us stay on the same page and saves us both time in the end.

JAMES: *What is most important as far as the Executive and Executive Assistant relationship is that no single tool is going to replace that relationship. It is impossible. Technology will never have feelings; will never recognize you are having a bad day; will never be a strategic partner. You really want that EA to grow into your strategic partner. A strategic partner will know when and how to effectively use technology. What the Executive and EA should do is say, "Which tools can be effectively utilized by either of us to enhance or fill in the gap or improve communication?"*

JOAN: *I can come across as not liking tech. That is not true. I wish I had some of these tools when I was an Executive Assistant. The challenge is that the options are overwhelming. Often Executives will ask me which is the best tech tool for them and their Executive Assistant to use to track their action items, do follow-up, and manage priorities. I work with clients all over the world and in a variety of industries, many of whom have their own internal preferences. I have not seen one particular application or platform become the industry standard tool of choice for Executives and Executive Assistants to use together. At the time of this writing, there is only one tool, Emmre, that I am aware of which was specifically designed for Executives and their EAs to use in tandem. I tell Executive Assistants and their Executives to try a few different tools and figure out what works best for them. Sometimes it is a combination of "old school" methods paired with new tech.*

JAMES: *I appreciate your point about not being anti-tech. You do not need ten applications. My suggestion for getting started in any of the* tech spaces is for the Executive to lean into their Executive Assistant to research it themselves. The Executive Assistant is going to know better than the Executive, more often than not, what tools are needed based on the research they do, the enhancements to the communication that are needed (such as where the holes are in the conversation), and their interaction styles.

JOAN: *When we talk about the value of an Executive Assistant, how many Executives run to their EAs and ask, "How do I do this? How do I do X?" There are so many times I call Melia into my office when boxes pop up on the screen while using Microsoft Word or Outlook. Often, they are pop ups I have not seen before, and I did not even touch anything! Sometimes, my screen goes black. It is not my job to figure it out, especially because I do not have the time. But Melia will figure it out. Executive Assistants will look at your device, or they will research it, or Google it, and they will fix it. Imagine the time and money that saves you!*

JAMES: *Agreed. This goes with the whole adding value piece. We, as Executives, do not really pay attention to how many times Executive Assistants are called upon in the technical realm. It is absolutely the wrong answer for IT to tell me (a fast-moving and demanding senior leader) to submit a Helpdesk ticket. Thank goodness for my Executive Assistant who can handle technology issues, who has the patience, and more importantly, once that ticket is submitted, can escalate it so that it receives the attention needed right away.*

I am not trying to break the IT processes to get special treatment, however, if I am working on something that the business needs to have move quickly, I cannot wait for a helpdesk ticket to get to IT to resolve the problem. My Executive Assistant pushes it forward and we make it happen. And my EA understands the prioritization of the needs for the organization because she has become a strategic partner. The strategy drives the prioritization so when we go back all the way to the intent of the Executive/Executive Assistant relationship, which is to become the strategic partners we need to be in order to be more effective together for our organization. Who better to lean into than your Executive Assistant?

Executive Assistant Talent: Moves Mountains

JAMES: *I would like to comment about power because power can be used or misused. When I think about an EA and their ability to "move mountains" when the intent and the empowerment is for the positive, it is magical. Things get done quickly, and the needs of the business, team, project move forward beautifully. On the negative side, the misuse of power could be detrimental. It is important that we go back to trust and that the Executive knows that the Executive Assistant means well, is aligned on vision, understands the strategy, and can utilize that power. Whether you want them to have it or not, they do have that power, and so it is really important for the Executive to have that trust in their Executive Assistant to move on their behalf.*

I do not know that you should spend time worrying about the power your EA has. You should just embrace it. Recognize that it is true, and keep that power focused on the important things so that you can advance your vision forward. For the Executive who needs to limit that power, you have to pull back and communicate. If you come back to your objectives, your goals, and your visions, and then you can make sure that you have alignment. Then that power can be enhanced and embraced. A great Executive Assistant understands that their network is a tool in addition to the technological tools. The best tool we have are the people in our organizations.

JOAN: *It is even the little things. When I was an Executive Assistant, I built many relationships with caterers and event planners. I assisted in planning company picnics, client entertainment, and department holiday parties. I had good relationships with vendors from whom I ordered special gifts, flower, cheese and wine baskets, and even stationery. Because I had this vast external network, I could reach out and enlist help for my Executive's holiday parties or other events.*

JAMES: *An effective Executive does the exact same thing. It is the networks that make Executives effective; that is how we build our networks and how we connect with other Executives. The layering of that web is what makes the relationship so powerful. The Executive Assistant weaves it and the Executive weaves it. If we do so at the same time, the fibers overlap and become really strong.*

Allow Your Executive Assistant To Own Something They Are Passionate About

JAMES: *Joan, what do you think about an Executive allowing their EA to own something they are passionate about?*

JOAN: *One of the Executive Assistants, who attended one of my courses works for a Fortune 100 corporation, partners with a top-level Executive. This EA told me, "You know what I love about my Executive? She is letting me own something within the business that I am passionate about!"*

JAMES: *The fact that you can use the term "passion" in any component of the business is a very good thing. If you have an individual in any position, you should embrace their focus, energy, and passion on any topic because you are going to get exponential impact when you do that. Conversely, if you limit their opportunity to participate* *in something they are passionate about, they are going to potentially either lose that passion or apply it somewhere else which might be outside of your organization.*

I think it is absolutely foolish to not embrace someone's passion. And frankly, if it is something that I am not passionate about and they are, that's perfect. That means I do not have to do it and they are going to do it to the best of their abilities. When you bring that back around to the Executive/EA relationship, I think it is important to allow the EA and encourage the EA to find something that they are passionate about and let them drive it. This embraced passion and empowerment gives energy to the business in a way that you can capitalize on to make "win-win-win" situations: a win for you, a win for them, and a win for the organization, a real trifecta.

JOAN: *Later in my administrative career, I offered to create and teach short classes for the Executive Assistants in the company. I did not expect extra money, nor did I use company time to create the materials. That was interesting because growing up, I always wanted to be a teacher. I would play school every day after school. But then in my junior year of high school I went into the secretarial track. I fully embraced shorthand, typing, and operating office equipment. You see, I ultimately combined two loves: teaching and the secretarial profession.*

I wrote a plan, list of benefits, and what I would teach and enthusiastically presented it to my Executive. This happened in two different companies. My Executives were pleased that I took the initiative to provide some training for our support staff. Everyone won! Me, the EAs, and the company! In taking on that assignment, I developed many skills which I could also use in my job: problem solving, creativity, organizational skills, communication skills, and strategic thinking.

JAMES: *To me, the important part in this is that you went with a passion, a drive, and a plan to your Executive and outlined how your passion could be applied in a way that was positive for the business. If any of my employees bring something like that to my desk, I am almost certainly going to approve it and push it forward because anybody who puts that much thought into the context of an effort that they want to champion is most certainly going to champion in a successful way.*

However, if I have to go to an employee, suggest, direct, coach, and then mentor through all of the infrastructure necessary to accomplish a goal, I am less inclined to support the initiative.

It is also important to note that if an Executive believes that the EA is only there to serve them, they are stuck in a couple of generations ago because in today's modern economy, that Executive Assistant can add value anywhere they want in any organization.

Inclusion

When should you include your EA? When should you not? It is much easier to say than to do … you should include your EA as much as you can.

JAMES: *I believe that it is the Executive's responsibility to define the role of the Executive Assistant appropriately and concisely. That is not to say that the EA does not have a say in the roles and responsibilities, but the Executive is the hiring manager and thus, must be clear about the demands of the job. That said, the EA should always circle back to the Executive to verify that the role is as it seems. Specifically, the EA should circle back to see which meetings they should attend, ask about what role the EA should take in a meeting or task,* and also confirm upon completion of responsibilities and tasks, to demonstrate understanding and conclusion of initiative. I include my EA in staff meetings, project management meetings, Executive planning sessions and even Executive retreats. She is there to assist with the meetings, but also to participate in most of them as well. I will explicitly include her and invite her to participate either before the meeting or during the meeting. Sometimes though, I will just ask her to "listen for what is not being said." I may ask her to watch for body language or to listen for specific issues that I may not catch during the heat of the meeting.

Interestingly, I have heard Executives tell their EAs to stay at their desk while they are out of office to "keep the home fires burning." I suggest that although that can be an important role for the EA, they may be missing important inclusion during the out of office Executive meetings. Instead, put your #2 Executive in charge in your absence and bring your strategic partner (EA) to your meetings to increase effectiveness and impact.

Meetings

JAMES: *It is important to recognize there are many types of meetings. Some meetings should have just been an email or a text message. If you are diligent in meeting management, you will realize that your Executive Assistant may need to take meeting minutes and record the content of a meeting while in other meetings you need a fly on the wall. As the leading Executive, I have defined three levels of meeting intent that I communicate with my Executive Assistant. By defining and using these differentiations, you and your EA are aligned, and you ensure inclusion of your EA everywhere from providing administrative function all the way to strategic partner. Not every meeting is a strategic partnership kind of meeting, so it is important to maintain this explicit dialogue for clarity.*

JOAN: *As the EA, if you were inviting me to one of those defined level meetings, and it is my first attendance at that kind of meeting, how would you state your expectations on the role you wanted me to play?*

JAMES: *Before we had our first meeting, I would explain my concept of meeting levels, so you understood the expectations for your participation.*

- ***Administrative Function – Level 1.*** *If you as the EA will be in the meeting room, and perhaps you are recording it, preparing it, and taking action, that is an administrative function, not a partnership function. I will often invite my Executive Assistant in for a meeting like that by saying, "Hey, we are at 'Level 1' here. We need to take notes, make sure we capture all the of the content, and then circulate that out for additional communication."*

- ***Observer Role – Level 2.*** *I could also invite my Executive Assistant into a meeting because I need her to watch for something that I cannot watch for while I am running the meeting. I will ask for body language analysis. I will ask for an extra set of ears to listen for other problems that might be coming my way; the train that is heading my way I do not see coming, because that is part of my partnership with my EA. I need my EA watching my back. I can only be pointed in one direction at a time. If my EA partner is looking for things that I cannot see, that is very helpful.*

- ***Active Participant/Strategic Partner – Level 3.*** *I will often ask my EA to participate in the conversation. I want her to dive in with the team when we do our annual strategic planning session. My Executive Assistant will be an active participant. If she is not speaking up, I will nudge her and say, "Hey, you need to step it up." I will ask her to participate at a higher level if she is being too quiet. If she is speaking too much, I will tell her to "pull back"* *a little bit to let the other participants speak, too. The Executive Assistant is an extension of me so if I am in the room but cannot participate in a given conversation, my EA should be able to handle that for me and understand the needs of the organization.*

JAMES: *Context is important. It is so powerful to say to your Executive Assistant:*

> *"This group of people is extremely important to our organization. I would like to send them a clear, nonverbal message that they are important to us. One of the best compliments I can offer to them, and to you as the Executive Assistant, is to designate you as the person whose job it is to be available to support them."*

The trust that an Executive must have to ask that Executive Assistant to do that task is immense. You are saying to the EA that they are the best person in the organization to help me send this message to the client. However, without the clear context, this task may have seemed menial. Perhaps a less effective Executive would say:

> *"Please go get these guys some coffee and when you get back, get their lunch orders. We will have our meetings while you are out."*

Think about it for a second: without context, is the EA going to stay in the "tactical" mindset or start to shift to the "strategic" frame of mind? Which mode do you prefer your EA to work from? Where do you get the most value from your EA, tactical or strategic?

There is a lot of power in having your Executive Assistant available. If an Executive can explain the context of the strategy to their EA partner, the initiative has more likelihood for success. I AM NOT saying you should explain every detail, each nuance and/or all the specifics associated with your initiatives, however, as the Executive, you SHOULD slow down enough to offer clear context. A strong EA/ strategic partner will fill in a lot of the details themselves once context is offered.

Belonging

*It is important that in the modern business world we have diversity, equity, equality, and inclusion (DEI). That is not enough in the modern business world though. We must encourage a **sense of belonging**. The sense of belonging is the feeling that you belong in the room, belong in the organization, and belong on the team. When you belong, it is YOUR team, too.*

By including your EA in your initiatives, bringing them into the strategic mindset for your meetings and providing adequate context for clarity, you are empowering your team. If you openly tell your team that your EA is an extension of you, then you are creating the sense of belonging. You should share your intent, openly address your EA's role and responsibility in an initiative, and finally, encourage the team to interact and engage with your EA in a manner that cements their sense of belonging with the team.

Avoid Micro-Managing

JAMES: *As you may be able to tell at this point, I am more of a macro-manager and tend to fail to provide adequate detail, sufficient clarity or necessary context. Thus far, many of my comments and guidance are for Executives like me, fast moving and "on to the next thing." The opposite Executive profile is dangerous, too.*

Let us address the micro-manager Executive. Many Executives are self-aware of this trait. I have found that if the Executive knows that they are micro-managing, they will acknowledge that it is a trust issue. When called to the mat, the Executive may say:

"I am micro-managing because I do not trust that the task will get done correctly, and it is important. Therefore, I must ensure it gets done by micro-managing or circling back continuously."

However, if the Executive is not aware that they are micro-managing, then it is a communication issue. It is a communication issue because they are having to come back and check in. They did not either give clear direction or a clear timeline, and the Executive Assistant is not communicating back.

The communication failure mode is much easier to fix than the trust failure mode. Figure out which one it is by testing your hypothesis through a "questioning" process.

Whoever is feeling the micro-management should ask themselves:
- Is this a trust issue or a communication issue?
- Have I failed to communicate or provide context?
- Have we skipped this topic in our huddle intentionally or unintentionally?
- Is there something that needs to be said that is being avoided?

Then, once you have determined which issue it is, you can go to work to fix it. The best way to resolve micro-management is to either improve communication or increase trust ... sometimes, to fully resolve, you may need to do both.

Two VERY different examples:

During a very significant business transaction, I feared that I was falling behind on email communication. Response time was criti-

cal to deal success, so I gave access and direction to my previous Executive Assistant to monitor email content. A few days in, I could tell that the stress of the responsibility was wearing on her and she started to become short and more brash than usual. I did not circle back to check in with her regularly, but during our daily huddle, it became clear that something was wearing on her. I asked, "What has changed since you started reading and monitoring my emails?" She responded, "I do not know how you do this. I have been reading these emails and now I cannot sleep at night. I feel like we are all doomed and there is nothing I can do." I asked her if any additional context or details would help her process the information differently, but she acknowledged that she could not get past some of the confidential information that she had learned. She began to act differently, and I began to treat her differently, by regularly checking in on her, asking for updates, and even personally completing assignments that I had given her to complete. This situation had evolved from a small communication issue to a huge trust issue; I felt that I could no longer trust her to serve as a strategic partner. Sadly, our relationship never recovered.

Sometime a few months later, and with a new Executive Assistant, I found myself deep in another confidential transaction. This time, I shared with my EA that the email frequency and complexity was catching up to me again. I did not ask her to monitor or track email correspondence this time, but instead, outlined ALL the other tasks and objectives on my "to do list." I outlined her on the goals, with prioritization. Since our relationship was new, I regularly checked back with her during the first few days, although I did not really have the time. Finally, she came to me and said: "James, I appreciate you checking in with me. I feel like you are micromanaging a little bit, and although I can handle it, I want you to know that you do not need to do this. I am committed to meeting the deadline that you asked for and to communicating back to you about that dead-line. When I finish the task, I will let you know. It will be on time and the quality will be as you have requested. Then, I will move to the next task assigned and do the same thing. I appreciate you carrying the weight of the transaction we are working on, and while you focus on that, I have got all these other items under control."

That was that. There was no longer a communication issue. More importantly, the trust building that our relationship needed was accelerated in a big way ... I knew that she would circle back to me if anything prevented her from completing a task or initiative. Although these two situations were different in nature and certainly in my own approach, you can see that the impact of the OUTCOME demonstrates that both communication and trust are key to the relationship between the EA and the Executive.

If my Executive Assistant gives me a status report update like that, I am done. I am going to move on to something else.

I would suggest to an Executive who is micromanaging to look inward and outward. You cannot just blame the Executive Assistant. Ask yourself, "Can better communication or trust building help fix this?" If it is communication that can help, make it happen. If it is trust building, do it. If trust has been lost and cannot be rebuilt, it is time to move on from this business relationship and begin a new one.

Your Assistant Has Needs Too

JOAN: *We have talked about the Executive this entire chapter. Executive Assistants have certain needs, too. If they are going to excel in their role and move that task or project forward, their needs have to be met. These are the common requests I hear from EAs:*

- *Need More Details.* *Your EA cannot read your mind. Do not make them pull information out of you. Instead, provide expectations about what you want the finished project to look like so they have a clear target to aim for. Provide boundaries or guard rails for what they should or should not do.*

- *Provide Clear Context.* *If you have travel, a meeting, a large project or an urgent initiative, provide context so the EA can be motivated to achieve success by knowing what the parameters are, what knowledge they need to acquire, they gather the correct tools, know where to start, and how often to check in with you to provide status updates.*

- *Clearer Direction.* *Do not think forwarding an email without expectations will provide enough direction or expect them to return to you over and over to progress to the next step. Provide clear direction.*

- *One-on-One.* *Be accessible to your EA to clarify expectations and perceptions, as necessary. Do not make them hunt you down to check in with you. Prioritize your EA as an extension of yourself.*

- *Expected Outcomes.* *Does your EA have a good grasp on your expectations?*

- *Open Communication.* *Are you open to your EA providing ideas and suggestions that could enhance the objectives?*

- *The Big Picture.* *Provide your EA with the big picture, not just tactical specifics.*

- *Communication Loop.* *Ensure your EA remains the center hub on the flow of information. Ask others to go through your*

EA, rather than pinging you directly, so the EA remains in the loop and aware of changing information.

- **Anticipation.** *If your EA knows what is "going on in your head" they can better anticipate and be proactive to help you.*

- **Discretion.** *Make it a point for you, as the Executive, and your EA, to operate with ethical discretion.*

SUMMARY

PART 4

James

- *Recognize that there is more than one way to get it done.*
- *Slow down to go fast.*
- *I would hate to have a strategic partner who was just like me. I want an EA strategic partner who balances me out and has the strengths where my weaknesses are; my weaknesses become their strengths.*
- *I realized that I have hired brilliant people who can perform this task to my liking and as needed for the business IF I get out of their way.*
- *Being able to perform a task yourself is powerful, but the issue with doing it yourself EVERY TIME is that you must do it EVERY TIME.*
- *The training and development of that [Executive/EA] relationship needs to be one of the most important components of an Executive's day because it represents who they are as an Executive.*
- *If I tag my EA in early enough and do the work up front to get that information flowing through her instead of me, then it saves me in the long run.*
- *It is also important to note that if an Executive believes that the EA is only there to serve them, they are stuck in a couple of generations ago because in today's modern economy, that Executive Assistant can add value anywhere they want in any organization.*

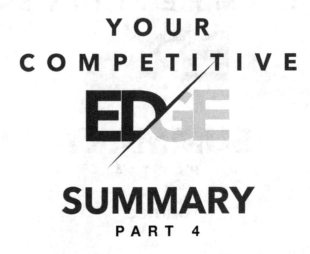

SUMMARY

PART 4

Joan

- *You do not know what you do not know.*
- *Utilizing the EA as a "center of influence" means everything flows through the Executive Assistant. Your EA becomes the central hub through which all information, strategies, goals, objectives, planning, communications, and such will flow.*
- *Have your Executive Assistant schedule a meeting for you with yourself so you can tie up loose ends each day, or on Friday for the following week.*
- *Ask yourself, "What areas of responsibility do I currently have that I would most like to see my EA handle?"*
- *Do not expect the same amazing results as if you put work into building a strategic partnership.*
- *Often the skills that people utilize in their personal life can be transferred to their professional life.*

- *It is no big deal to answer an email or schedule a meeting. Well, how many times a day or week are you doing that? Minutes add up to hours and weeks.*
- *Give on-the-spot feedback as to whether the work returned to you met your expectations and looked like you anticipated it would.*
- *What could you be spending your time on that has bigger impact than what you could delegate to your strategic partner?*

GEMS TO LEAD BY

PART 4

- An EA knows who is who.
- The sense of belonging is the feeling that you belong in the room, belong in the organization, and belong on the team. When you belong, it is YOUR team, too.
- Intentionally look for and analyze your EA's strengths.
- It can take as much as 6-12 months of building the foundation for a trusting relationship between an Executive and an EA to develop.
- Task switching is "expensive."
- Allow your EA to own something they are passionate about.
- The best way to resolve micromanagement is to either improve communication or increase trust ... sometimes, to fully resolve, you may need to do both.
- Executives do not really pay attention to how many times Executive Assistants are called upon in the technical realm.

WHY YOU NEED TO INVEST IN PROFESSIONAL DEVELOPMENT

The Executive's Competitive

EDGE

Learning in Tandem Leads to Growing in Tandem

JOAN: *Supporting your EA's professional development is a necessity, not a luxury. In the 21st century workplace, knowledge itself is now viewed as capital. It is vital for your EA to have the latest information, skills, and knowledge to be as effective as possible. Although historically EAs provided tactical services like typing, filing, taking meeting minutes, and arranging travel, now their role has evolved to a sophisticated service engaging higher-level thinking to better facilitate their strategic partnership with the management team.*

I knew that professional development for EAs was vital when I started Office Dynamics in 1990 on the premise that all assistants (Executive Assistants and Administrative Assistants) needed robust training to keep up with their growing Executives. The visual below represents the typical learning path for assistants. This path still exists today for many assistants because their organization or leader will not support their training. They believe assistants do not need training or do not want to invest the money in them.

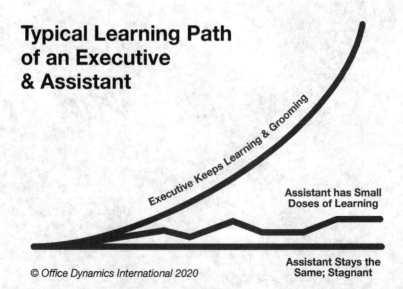

Typical Learning Path of an Executive & Assistant

Executive Keeps Learning & Grooming

Assistant has Small Doses of Learning

Assistant Stays the Same; Stagnant

Below is what the path should look like. When Executives and Executive Assistants learn in tandem they grow in tandem. The results to the team and organization are many. I listed a few in this visual.

Ideal Path: Executive & Assistant Learning in Tandem™

Leads to Growing in Tandem

- Effectively Manage Change
- De-escalation of Issues
- Increased Productivity
- Visionary Leadership
- Stronger Partnership
- Strategic Planning
- Engagement
- Less Stress
- Stability

The Executive

The Assistant

© Office Dynamics International 2020

JAMES: *This might be where the generational difference between you and me becomes more apparent in our styles. These graphics are intuitive in so much as they make me wonder who in the world would disagree with the concept that the Executive Assistant should grow in their career. If you take the Executive out of the picture and just show me a graphical representation of the Executive Assistant blipping across the X axis with moderate amounts of training here and there at random times, I will suggest there is something wrong with their employer and that person should look for a new role where they are appreciated.*

I believe that every team member should be growing in their role, for their own career and for their own professional development. I believe wholeheartedly that it is a key element of the Executive Assistant's job to support **their own** professional development and not the Executive's job to do this for them. Candidly, I can barely keep track of my own training, my own goals, and my own professional development; I do not have the energy or time to drive my Executive Assistant's growth. But it is my job to support my EA's growth, in tandem with my own. As she grows and develops, so does her ability to transfer value to our organization and our relationship.

JOAN: I want to respond to your generational difference comment. You are unique! You do "get it"! Unfortunately, still in this day and age, far too many companies and managers do not see the value or purpose in training their administrative staff or Executive Assistant. With that said, there are some amazing Fortune 500 companies who have invested thousands of dollars in training for their administrative community. They see the profession as integral to the organization; as a career with a path; and key to their leaders' successes. I have personally partnered with these organizations.

I agree that we need to drive our education and learning. I have always done that. My learning is more informal. I did not go to college, I was a self-learner everywhere, anywhere, every day. Whether I was reading or observing others in the workplace, I was filling my bag of skills. Not every employee thinks that way. The big issue is that organizations/management are not even thinking about pursuing training for their administrative staff. It is the farthest thing from their minds. That is why I was intrigued by you, James. You get it! You believe that Executive Assistants should get the training just like everyone else. So, if an organization believes in training their administrative staff, they are going to seek us out and hire us. And they will reap the benefits of that investment.

JAMES: My message to the Executive Assistant is that before you go *find a new company to work for because you feel unsupported, ask yourself if you have done your part. Have you made it clear that you want to grow with your Executive, and have you made it easy for them to say "Yes, go for it"?*

An Executive would be crazy to say "No" to this approach:

> *"I have identified the Star Achievement Series® for Executive Assistants. Here is the content from the coursework and I believe that as I learn these things, I will add more value and here are three reasons why."*

To the Executive that may not buy into this yet, you are in big trouble. For every one of you that does not support your EA, there are dozens of Executives looking for an EA with this level of communication and commitment to excellence.

I have heard only two arguments for NOT supporting the EA's professional development. The first argument is:

> *"The organization cannot afford to train the Executive Assistants."*

I am not even going to address this with data or validate its relevance with argument. I will just ask this: "Can the organization afford NOT training the Executive Assistants?" The second argument is:

> *"Once my Executive Assistant gets trained up, they will leave the organization for something better."*

And? You are right if you are not growing too, but your concern should not be with your EA in that case. If you are not growing, ALL your team will leave, and you will be asked to leave one day as well.

Grow in tandem. Support each other's professional development and show the cost of NOT supporting each other to anyone that challenges the financial implications of training. If you are an Executive and you value the relationship you have with the Executive Assistant as your partner, you will find the budget, you'll find the money, and you'll see it as an investment rather than as an expense. Investments sit on the balance sheet and not the income statement. You should figuratively see the training for your EA as a "balance sheet line" rather than a cost sitting on the P&L.

JOAN: *I understand an Executive may have a fear of making this investment because that EA may not stay with them for years to come. Many employees, in general, job hop. They jump to the next better, bigger, and higher paying opportunity. I have that same concern as a business owner. My thinking though is that there is value in the present moment. I receive something in return today! If you invest $1,200 for a three-day certification course for your EA, and that EA works with you for two years while operating at the top of their game, you are receiving dividends in return during those two years.*

And you really never lose because when that great EA leaves, you will know what to expect from your next EA. You will set your bar high and retain a higher caliber EA. You will not settle for mediocrity. It happened to one of my Executives during my EA career. I worked for him for 5 years. I grew during that time, and I taught my Executive how to work with a strategic partner. My husband then got a promotion that took us to another state. My Executive knew exactly what he wanted in his next EA.

JAMES: *That's a great point. Paraphrasing and summarizing for the Executive: when an Executive Assistant comes to training with Office Dynamics, they should be able to return to the office to train the Executive! For $5,000 in EA training, the EA gets to transfer that value to one* *or more people in the organization. The student becomes the teacher. You did not have to go to the class because the EA is going to find and filter the information from the training and bring it to the Executive and other support staff in an applicable, boiled down way.*

Joan, I am not sure if you have ever been told this, but via EA proxy, you are actually in the Executive Training space too!

Your Executive Assistant Must Optimize Current Skills and Learn New Skills

JOAN: *Below are reasons why Executive Assistants must attend training, continue to polish their current skills, learn new skills, and stretch out of their comfort zone.*

Unceasing Change
It is predicted that in the next 10 years we will experience more changes than in the past 10 years at an accelerated rate. Continual learning will ensure Executive Assistants are not left behind.

Molding Their Career
No one is handed a dream career "on a platter." Each individual needs to step up to create his or her desired career. They need to make informed decisions and be accountable for their own actions and the outcomes. Your EA can thrive in these paradigm shifts by developing their skills, attitudes, and team relationships beyond where they are today. Most importantly, your EA needs to create a realistic, workable, proactive, and positive strategy.

Competitive Marketplace
Now more than ever your company needs Executive Assistants to contribute to the organization by producing quality work, being a

team player, improving work processes, and sharing their knowledge. They need to do more than show up: they need to contribute! Many organizations are doing more work with fewer people. The people who are on the job must help their organization remain competitive by keeping their skills current and being the best they can be.

Pace at Which We Work

The hypersonic fast-paced workplace pace of work demands that we be alert, sharp, inquisitive, and thought leaders who anticipate issues and have solutions ready at hand. Every employee is expected to be creative and innovative. Because of the importance and level of the Executives supported by the Executive Assistants, they need to be more focused, more resilient, better prepared for anything that comes their way, and masters of time and energy.

Senior Executives Have Higher Expectations of Administrative Staff

While there has been a big shift over recent years with EAs supporting more than one leader, senior Executives are raising the bar higher. As Executives are seeing the value an EA can bring to the table, they are raising their expectations thus challenging the EA to strive for increased excellence.

Build Confidence

Executive Assistants are not always as confident as the leadership they support. When an EA is prepared with the right tools and support, their confidence increases, which pours over everything they do.

Personal Satisfaction Leading to Happier Lives

Executive Assistants who attend training specific to their career and needs, transfer the concepts, strategies, skills, and techniques to their personal lives, with outstanding results. They create higher success and satisfaction in their personal life in many ways; they meet financial goals, reduce debt, decrease stress, enjoy better health, plan family vacations, and utilize their artistic passions. This transfers back to their professional role, creating a win-win.

Be a Catalyst for Cultural Change

JOAN: *I want to be completely authentic here because developing Executive Assistants and their Executives is near and dear to my heart. It has been my passion since 1990. It is important to me to align an Executive Assistant's pace of growth with that of their Executive and management team, and to improve the quality of their work life.*

Administrative-specific training was not available nor heard of in 1990. Leaders and organizations had a litany of reasons why Executive Assistants did not need training or why they would not invest in the training. However, I was able to make a difference and help them understand why training their staff was important. By the mid-90s, several large corporations were reaching out to me to provide training as they realized this community of employees had been overlooked far too long. They also realized providing training and development led to retention, employee satisfaction, and groomed Executive Assistants to assume higher-level EA roles in the future. These companies were building a pipeline for the VPs and C-Suite Executives who could not afford any downtime by hiring an outsider.

How To Support Your Executive Assistant's Development

There are several ways for Executives to support their EA's professional development. Here are a few to consider:

1. ***Encourage it!*** *To me, this is the first step. Do not wait for your EA to come to you. I hope you will discuss this when mapping goals for the new year or assisting them with their individual development plans. Be your EA's champion! They need you in their corner.*

2. ***Identify growth areas.*** *Your EA will have a good feel for where they want to develop. As an Executive, though, you see areas where your assistant can grow. Remember the Johari Window in an earlier chapter? You need to identify their blind spots.*

3. ***Invest Financially.*** *Allocate an annual education budget for your EA. While I often tell Executive Assistants to invest in their own education if their company will not support them, I know it is difficult for EAs to find the funds to attend conferences or certification courses that are upwards of $1,000.*

   Years of experience in this industry has shown me that companies will readily pay for training for Executives, managers, salespeople, customer service, marketing, and other job roles. When it comes to an Executive Assistant, the EA has to jump through hoops to justify the training and prove the ROI. This is just not right. One EA who supported a CEO spent three years trying to convince the CEO to bring in our flagship training program, The Star Achievement Series® to their organization. Fortunately, she was persistent and determined. Finally, the CEO said "Yes," and that program is still being taught today to not only the Executive Assistants but to other job roles, like wealth management.

4. ***Set your expectations.*** *I take training seriously. I expect to see behavior change. I set a high bar for my students. I know you or the organization are making an investment and you expect a return. So, set your expectations high for what you want to see when your EA has finished the*

training. It is helpful to have that conversation before your EA attends training or a conference or takes an extensive online course.

5. **Give your EA time to attend training, without guilt.** Whether your EA needs an hour to attend a webinar or three-day conference, give them that time willingly. Some Executives make their EA feel so guilty for not being available and it is not fair to the EA. Other times, EAs will not even ask their Executive if they can attend training because they do not want to leave them hanging by themselves for a few days. Look at those three days as an investment in your future.

6. **Be open to trying new things your EA has learned.** When Executive Assistants attend my training, I expect them to implement what they learn. Sometimes an EA will tell me they tried to "build a strategic partnership" or tried to "be more assertive" or tried to "manage their Executive's calendar," but hit a brick wall. Their Executive did not want it.

7. **Have check-ins.** If your EA is attending a series of trainings, such as we offer, check-in between the training sessions for growth and progress.

8. **Be curious!** When your EA has just attended a webinar or workshop, ask them "What three things stood out for you the most?" or "What three things did you learn that you are going to implement right away?"

9. **Hold your EA accountable.** Most often you have made a financial investment in the training, so hold your EA accountable for execution. Of course, you have to know what they were supposed to be learning to do that. If your EA has attended a conference, have your EA report back. We have had several EAs over the years who attended our World Class Assistant certification course or annual conference and who following the training, created a PowerPoint presentation for their Executive to share what they learned and how those learnings would be implemented.

What Kind of Training Does Your Executive Assistant Need?

JOAN: *Earlier in this book, James wrote about tactical and strategic work. For decades, being in the training industry, I have referred to these as foundation and advanced competencies. New EAs need to learn the foundation skills. But even seasoned EAs need to polish their foundation skills as that is what they use almost every day and things are constantly changing.*

In the model to the right:

- *I listed the top 15 foundation competency areas. While the original list was developed several years ago, I updated the competency areas at the writing of this book to incorporate competencies necessary for our post-pandemic world.*

- *I identified some of the significant advanced competencies assistants need to excel in the profession and be a strong strategic partner. The Star Approach™ is from Office Dynamics' flagship training program, the Star Achievement Series®. Star-achieving assistants synergize these four components into their everyday professional performance and, over time, fully develop as leaders who exhibit confidence at work, at home, and in the community.*

    - ***Attitude:*** *achieving and sustaining a positive attitude about your employer, your coworkers, your clients, and yourself.*
    - ***Skill:*** *developing new and enhancing current intangible skills that are vital to workplace success.*
    - ***Teamwork:*** *being part of and contributing to various team relationships, both internal and external to the organization.*
    - ***Strategy:*** *setting goals and cultivating enriching relationships to actualize your professional self.*

Star-Performing Administrative Professional Competency Model

This rich combination of attitude, skill, teamwork and strategy leads to performance excellence and career success.

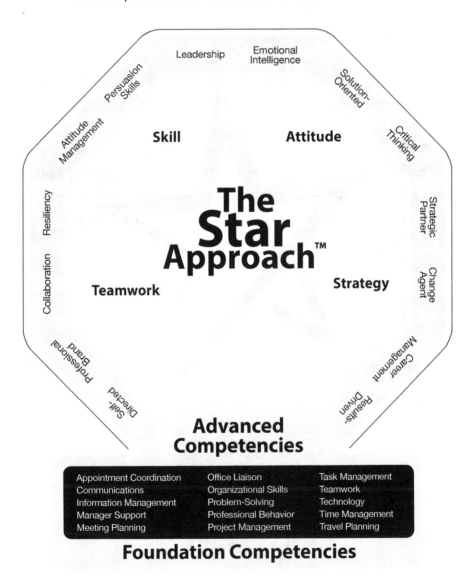

© Office Dynamics International 2013; 2022

Coaching for You, the Executive

JOAN: *If you have gotten this far in the book, congratulations! You have learned best practices on how to work with an EA. Your learning does not stop here. I encourage you to get coaching with an industry expert who knows the ins and outs of this special work partnership. I am sure you know that when you work with a coach, they learn about you, your specific needs, and will then customize your coaching sessions to address those needs. This is the real beauty of working with a coach.*

JAMES: *As Joan said, Congratulations, you are almost to the end of the book. But wait, there is more! You are not getting out of here without working on yourself a bit! Be sure to capitalize on the opportunity to train WITH your EA. You can only hope to be half as good as your EA is!*

SUMMARY

PART 5

James

- *Work on yourself a bit!*
- *Every team member should be growing in their role, for their own career and for their own professional development.*
- *It is my job to support my EA's growth, in tandem with my own.*
- *My message to the Executive Assistant is that before you go find a new company to work for because you feel unsupported, ask yourself if you have done your part.*
- *Capitalize on the opportunity to train WITH your EA.*

YOUR COMPETITIVE EDGE

SUMMARY

PART 5

Joan

- *In the 21st century workplace, knowledge itself is now viewed as a product. It is vital for your EA to have the latest information, skills, and knowledge to be as effective as possible.*
- *The EA role has evolved to a sophisticated service engaging higher-level thinking to better facilitate their strategic partnership with the management team.*
- *Your EA can thrive in these paradigm shifts by developing their skills, attitudes, and team relationships beyond where they are today.*
- *Now more than ever your company needs Executive Assistants to contribute to the organization by producing quality work, being a team player, improving work processes, and sharing their knowledge.*
- *Whether your EA needs an hour to attend a webinar, or a three-day conference, give them the time willingly.*

GEMS TO LEAD BY

PART 5

- You should figuratively see training for your EA as a "balance sheet line" rather than a cost sitting on the P&L.
- As Executives are seeing the value an EA can bring to the table, they are raising their expectations thus challenging the EA to strive for increased excellence.
- The student becomes the teacher.
- Executive Assistants who attend training specific to their career and needs, transfer the concepts, strategies, skills, and techniques to their personal lives, with outstanding results.
- Be your EA's champion!
- When your EA has just attended a webinar or workshop, ask them "What three things stood out for you the most?" or "What three things did you learn that you are going to implement right away?"
- Executives gain a Competitive Edge when their Executive Assistants, who are educated, skilled and trained, operate at the highest level of excellence:
    - Outstanding work quality.
    - Anticipates Executive's needs.
    - Steers clear of petty office squabbles.
    - Works with integrity and discretion.

- Reduces expense wherever possible.
- Performs well under pressure.
- Confident, exhibits a positive brand.
- Solves problems and/or provides solutions.
- Keeps the office rolling forward in a positive, productive way.
- Will ask for additional challenges and new responsibilities because they feel confident.
- Meeting management and office management skills will be enhanced.
- Have the confidence necessary to present at department or organizational meetings.
- Meeting participation will increase with viable ideas and contributions.

LOOKING FOR A STAR PERFORMER

The Executive's
Competitive
EDGE

JOAN: *I have been fortunate over the years to meet incredible managers, leaders, and Executives. I have learned as much from them as they have from me. In 2022, I met Don Harms (see insert box). Like James Bristow, Don fully understands the importance of value of a strategic partnership. Don often speaks to Executives on why they need to enlist an EA and how to effectively work with that person. I believe his "1 Job, 2 People Mindset" sets the stage in helping Executives and HR professionals for the hiring process.*

1 Job, 2 People Mindset

"When an Executive hires a strategic partner to assist them, they aren't creating a new distinct role. They are just getting help to accomplish the role they already have. The Executive Assistant is responsible for helping the Executive better achieve the goals, objectives, projects, and results that are part of the Executive's role."

—**Don Harms**, Founder & CEO, Emmre

Not Just Anyone Can Be a Stellar Executive Assistant!

Not all Executive Assistants are equal; just as not all Executives are equal. I have been teaching EAs how to be Star performers in their roles and work since 1990. I know what it takes to be a Star assistant; what it takes to shine, to stand out, to excel, and deliver the highest level of assistance and customer service. I have been fortunate to train and work with stellar Executive Assistants.

When I started Office Dynamics and was determining what I would teach Executive Assistants, I thought back to my 20 years in the administrative profession working in 12 different companies, and wondered, "Why did certain Executive Assistants stand out where others did not? What made those Executive Assistants shine?" I made a long list of the attributes, qualities, attitudes, and skills of the Star assistants. From there I bundled them into four main components: attitude, skill, teamwork, and strategy. (Eventually this led me to creating our flagship training program, the Star Achievement Series®)

The DNA of a Star Assistant

What are the qualities, attributes, attitudes, and behaviors of Star assistants? Why do certain Executive Assistants stand out and shine brighter than others? Are Star assistants created or is it their innate abilities that allow them to be Stars? Are there certain qualities and traits a person needs to be successful working at the top echelons in the company? After working with and studying administrative professionals for 50 years, I can respond with confidence. We have data that supports the theory that Stars are born. This is not to suggest this is the entire story, but it is a breakthrough discovery and one that can help you be more selective in your hiring choices. This may very well change your entire future.

A person is wired or not wired for certain things. It is in your DNA. For example, one Executive Assistant naturally has the talent to connect the dots when given abstract information where another does not.

Or one EA is highly creative, and another is not; another is skilled at thinking of the details, and another is not.

I remember when I was an Executive Assistant to the CEO of a large bank in Memphis, Tennessee. I had only been with him about 9 months and then my husband was promoted and accepted a job in another state. My CEO was very disappointed but gracious. We interviewed several EAs and finally hired someone to support him. I remember he said to me, "She is a diamond in the rough." Meaning, she had good skills but needed polishing. I can similarly say that certain EAs have a core base of talent and they can easily excel in certain areas of their role. But even Stars need to continually elevate. This is where professional development comes into play.

As far as hiring someone, you want to find an individual who naturally has those core talents or gifts or has had extensive experience in the field. Quite honestly, I am shocked when I get a call from an HR Director who tells me they hired someone with no prior experience to be an Executive Assistant for their CEO or a top-tier Executive. The EA is usually fresh out of college, but not always. Those individuals should go into entry-level administrative work, not support a top Executive. They simply do not have the experience in the field or the business world. I am not saying they cannot be taught. My question to Executives is, "Are you at a level in your career where you need a strategic partner vs. a task doer?" Then you need to raise your expectations for the experience level of the EA you are hiring.

The Interview: What To Look for; What To Run From

There is no greater partnership in the business world than that of an Executive and the Executive Assistant providing support and strategic partnership. A Star-performing EA can save you time, handle your projects, reduce your workload, act as a liaison between you and your staff or other departments, help you get organized, act as a buffer, and is worth their weight in gold. When you have the "right" business partner, you reduce turnover, stress, and can excel in your own career. Therefore, it would behoove you to invest time when interviewing for this position. While I do not have a magic formula for you, I can provide some specific guidelines that I have used in hiring my own Executive Assistants.

Before the Interview

Before you write an advertisement, post a job internally or externally, or interview one candidate, be very clear on what you expect of this person and the qualities that are important to you. Aside from listing the skills required to do the job or the tasks that will be performed in that job, you need to consider what attributes, values, and behaviors you want the successful candidate to embody. I know one high-level Executive who must have an Executive Assistant who is professional personified—from head to toe! Another Executive I know needs an EA who can always maintain calmness, and another one needs an Executive Assistant who has outstanding customer service skills.

If you do not take the time to think this through and make your list, you will have turnover and continue to waste your time bringing a new Executive Assistant up to speed. Also, determine if you require a Personal Assistant in conjunction with the Executive Assistant, or only an Executive Assistant. It is important to be upfront about this during the interview, as some EAs do not want to be involved in managing the personal side.

Depending on your level within your organization, your needs may be slightly different than what I am providing here. At minimum, you want an Executive Assistant with five years of experience.

Skills

I bet you may think this profession is all about technical skills. Our 30+ years of ongoing research proves differently. Every time we ask Human Resource professionals, Training & Development, managers, Executives, CEOs, and Executive Assistants, "What skills, attitudes, and behaviors are necessary to succeed in this profession?" The list contains 90% interpersonal/intrapersonal skills and only 10% technical expertise. It makes sense. While EAs leverage technology all day, people are behind the technology. And to determine which technology to use and how it interfaces with process flow, they have to use their brains!

Every great Executive Assistant needs to be excellent at the foundation skills because these are the skills they use every day. What am I referring to?
- *Tech savvy*
- *Excellent communication skills*
- *Organizational skills*
- *Time and project management*
- *Appointment scheduling and meeting planning*
- *Travel planning experience*
- *Professional presence*
- *Attention to detail*
- *Ability to follow up and follow through*
- *Ability to prioritize without direction all the time*
- *Good grammar and proofreading*

Attitudes/Traits/Behaviors
- *Ethical*
- *Discreet*
- *Flexible*
- *Ability to remain calm under pressure*
- *Self-motivated/self-starter*

- *Hungry to learn*
- *Anticipates problems*
- *Accountable*
- *Good listener*
- *Curiosity*
- *Approachable*
- *Team player*
- *Positive, "can do" attitude*
- *Dependable*

And there is more—way too many to list so I have provided what I would expect as a minimum. Again, what is important to you based on your role, and who you are as an individual?

During the Interview

As a savvy Executive, I am sure you know several guidelines to interviewing. Use many of the same tactics as you would for hiring any person for your team. Additionally, seek a candidate who is creative in their approach to the interviewing process and an individual who learned about your organization prior to the interview.

Situational interviewing will be your best approach to determining the soft skills. Two and a half years ago, I changed my entire approach to my interviewing process for an Executive Assistant and have been extremely happy in my selection. My process included three pages of items. Below, I have provided a sampling of my list.

Situational/Behavioral

- *Executive Assistants must manage sensitive or challenging situations with savvy. Describe an example of how you managed a sensitive or challenging work situation well, and the outcome.*

- *Describe a situation where your "focus on the future" as an EA has had a positive outcome for your Executive or your business.*

- *Explain one way that you have either saved money or generated income for an employer.*

- *A team member or Executive approaches you with a suggestion on how to improve your performance. How do you react?*

- *Your Executive is out of the office and completely unable to be reached, and someone calls with a critical issue that must be handled immediately. What do you do? (Looking for an answer that says the EA would learn the Executive's preferences/expectations in advance and make the best decision or defer to other Executives within the company.)*

- *Your Executive asks you to schedule a virtual meeting. You are the first person to join. Do you go on camera or not? What might you display in the meeting space? As people join the meeting, what do you do, particularly if your Executive has not joined yet? How would you provide pre-reads or agenda within the meeting application? Are you competent to use the chat feature within the meeting?*

Skills

- *Demonstrate your proficiency in Microsoft Teams, SharePoint, Word, Excel, PowerPoint, and virtual tools. (Looking for a portfolio here. Also, we might tell them in advance we are looking for proof of their technical skills prior to the on-site interview.)*

- *Do you have a career portfolio, or anything that demonstrates your abilities?*

- *What system do you use for follow-up on important items and time-critical tasks?*

- *What system do you use for managing emails – yours and your Executive's emails?*

- *What do you think it means to manage your Executive's calendar holistically?*

Traits

- *Office Dynamics is a progressive, growing training and development company focused on customer service, sales, and a stellar professional image. Describe the scope of your job within a company like this.*

- *How important is career advancement to you? What are some of the ways an Executive Assistant to the CEO could "advance" meaningfully within a company in order to enjoy job satisfaction long-term?*

- *Tell us one way in which you have become a "value-added partner" for your current employer. (Value-added meaning just that – you have added value to your company.)*

- *Define how you and your work impacts your Executive's success.*

- *If you are having a "bad day" how do you typically manage that?*

- *How important to your success is building a network of professional contacts?*

Possible Practical Evaluations
**(Grade them from 1 to 5 – one being least skilled,
5 being highly skilled.)**

- *Speaking skills.* This could be a three-minute speech on-site in which the person talks about him/herself, the honors and awards received, or whatever else we prefer. Demonstrates ability to present oneself as well as image.

- *Email skills.* Have one of our team evaluate email skills by emailing the applicant to ask a few questions. Review the reply to ensure it meets our standards, and note how quickly the candidate replied.

- *Writing skills.* Submit one piece of writing (a letter written for an Executive, etc.) for review. (Also, send several of the questions above as an email and request a response.)

- *Proofreading skills.* Give the applicant a document riddled with grammatical and spelling errors and see how well (and how quickly) they edit and correct the document.

- *Presentation building skills.* Create a deck of at least 3 slides to be presented at a department meeting of managers and staff on the topic of reducing stress at work. Include speaking notes, graphics, and an eye-catching cover.

- *Diversity and Inclusion skills.* Request the candidate provide a recent example of their involvement in the D&I initiatives at their current job. What have they done in the past 12 months to increase their D&I knowledge and awareness? How have they helped someone by creating a tailwind (helping them be included or move forward) instead of a headwind (making it harder or taking no action if they are not assimilating easily into the team)?

Follow-up Interviews

Once you select your top two or three candidates, bring those individuals back at least twice; even a third time is advisable. If possible, meet them individually in a different environment, such as a restaurant for a luncheon. This way you can see how each presents themselves outside the office environment. Have two – three of your staff members meet with these individuals to provide you with their perspectives.

Talk to the candidates on the telephone to see how they handle themselves, to check their voice modulation, and their vocabulary when they need to "think on their feet."

Initiate a virtual meeting to gain a sense of how they present themselves to others. Do they sound monotone? Professional? Enthusiastic? Look like they just rolled out of bed? Ask them if they can tell you what elements they would include on a virtual meeting agenda.

At this stage, additional items you want to look for are the depth and range of their past responsibilities and work background. This person will usually be more well-rounded. I like to know their involvement outside of work, any leadership roles, committee work, etc. This gives me a feel for how involved this person is and especially demonstrates that they are a person of action.

Stay Away From

I have seen my share of Executive Assistants over the years. Because I intimately know this profession, I recommend you stay away from anyone who ...

- *Is late for the interview.*
- *Keeps changing times or day of their interview.*
- *Appears to lack confidence.*

- *Demonstrates any habits that annoy you.*
- *Is only interested in how soon they can move out of the administrative profession.*
- *Looks like they are going to the supermarket, gym, or local nightclub.*
- *Submits a resume that is:*
    - *Sloppy*
    - *Generic/cloned*
    - *Contains typos or improper grammar and punctuation*
    - *Not formatted appropriately (they do not pay attention to details)*
    - *Incorrect verb tense or verb tense changes throughout the resume. You will have problems with this person using correct tense when corresponding on your behalf or representing your organization*
    - *Lack initiative and only show they are a "task doer"*
    - *Check their social media presence on Facebook, Instagram, YouTube, and LinkedIn. Do their posts, photos and other elements blend with your company's public presence?*

You are Hired!

Once you have hired the right person, you want to do everything you can to keep that great Executive Assistant. This is a relationship you will want to develop. Nurture your EA by providing challenging assignments, supporting their training and development, and encouraging and allowing them to join a professional organization to support them in their role.

Need an EA Search Firm?

At Office Dynamics International, we do not get involved in recruiting and interviewing Executive Assistants. Our focus is on assessing strengths and weaknesses, coaching, and training. We also have Executive Assistant Competency Assessments.

I personally recommend two EA-specific search firms. I have known the founders for years and can vouch for their level of excellence and service. They fully understand the roles and scope of the Executive Assistant and Chief of Staff.

- *East Coast (New York): Melba Duncan, CEO of The Duncan Group; duncangroupinc.com*

- *West Coast (California): Leni Miller, CEO of EA Search, LLC; easearch.com*

YOUR COMPETITIVE EDGE

SUMMARY
PART 6
Joan

- *A person is wired or not wired for certain things. It is in their DNA.*
- *Office Dynamics bundles the attributes, qualities, attitudes, and skills of Star assistants into four main components: attitude, skill, teamwork, and strategy.*
- *Situational interviewing will be your best approach to assessing a candidate's soft skills.*
- *When hiring, look for the depth and range of past responsibilities and work background.*
- *Carefully review the resume to see the quality of the candidate's writing and proofreading skills.*
- *Once you select your top two or three candidates, bring those individuals back at least twice to see them in multiple environments, such as a restaurant.*
- *Ask your staff to provide input on the candidates through brief "meet and greets" with the top candidates.*
- *How involved is this person in the community? Does the candidate demonstrate that they are a person of action?*
- *Nurture your EA by providing challenging assignments and supporting their training and development.*

JOAN'S FINAL WORD TO EXECUTIVES

If you read this entire book, I commend you! James and I are grateful for the time you took to broaden your knowledge and embrace some new ideas. I hope you are motivated by the material in this book and have discovered ways to apply these principles in your workplace.

I once heard a wise businessman say, "Education without implementation is just entertainment." Now, it is time for you to execute! Don't waste one more day using your precious energy on tasks you should not be doing. Find that amazing EA. If you already have an EA, create the strategic partnership we discussed in this book.

If you would like additional one-on-one guidance specific to your partnership or organization, please reach out to me at 800-STAR-139.

With gratitude and appreciation,

Joan Burge
CEO and Founder
Office Dynamics International

APPENDIX

The Executive's
Competitive

EDGE

ADDITIONAL RESOURCES

1. *The Founder & The Force Multiplier: How Entrepreneurs and Executive Assistants Achieve More Together* by Adam Hergenrother and Hallie Warner. ISBN-10: 0578439891

2. Johari Window, created in 1955 by Joseph Luft and Harry Ingham. See https://en.wikipedia.org/wiki/Johari_window.

3. *The CEOs Secret Weapon: How Great Leaders and Their Assistants Maximize Productivity and Effectiveness* by Jan Jones. ISBN-10: 1137444231

4. The Evolving Executive by Dana Wilkie, article published on the Society for Human Resource Management (SHRM) website, February 26, 2022

5. Creating a Hybrid Culture: 5 Things Employees Need Now, article published at Steelcase website

6. BetterUp Labs 64-page Report / Winter 2022

7. Will the Metaverse Affect Human Relationships? - A Tech with Heart Episode with Michelle Calloway, published November 11, 2021

8. *The Speed of Trust: The One Thing That Changes Everything*, by Stephen Covey. ISBN-10: 1416549005

9. The Cost of Multitasking: How Much Productivity Is Lost Through Task Switching? By Ian Hanes, published October 21, 2021

BOOKS BY JOAN BURGE

1. *Executives and Assistants Working In Partnership: The Definitive Guide to Success*

2. *Joan's Greatest Administrative Secrets Revealed*

3. *Become An Inner Circle Assistant*

4. *Underneath It All: How Top-Tier Executive Assistants Create a Competitive Advantage*

5. *Survival Guide for Secretaries and Administrative Assistants*

6. *Who Took My Pen ... Again? Secrets from Dynamic Executive Assistants*

7. *Give Yourself Permission to Live A BIG Life*

ABOUT THE AUTHORS

JAMES BRISTOW, PE, Managing Partner at Universal Engineering Sciences, is a highly educated and credentialed leader in engineering sciences. His writing balances extensive thought leadership with an unabashed openness to share real-world experiences about how to best manage the Executive/Executive Assistant strategic partnership.

James became the owner and CEO of his own Las Vegas engineering firm at the age of 28. He grew the company and in 2020, James' firm joined the Universal Engineering Sciences Family of Companies. James is now responsible for expanding the Western Division of the nation's fastest-growing engineering firm.

Throughout this time, James has been a constant student at UNLV. Earning his master's degree and is currently working towards his Ph.D. in engineering. He is also an active member of several boards for industry organizations, such as the Nevada Contractor's Association, American Concrete Institute (ACI), American Society for Testing and Materials (ASTM), and more. His career experiences constantly push him to "pay it forward" and encourage the next generation of leaders to excel and challenge themselves.

 **JOAN BURGE**, Founder and CEO of Office Dynamics International, is a well-respected global industry leader and known as the pioneer of the administrative training industry. After working 20 years in the administrative profession, Joan created a business in an untapped niche, overcoming monumental obstacles involving corporations' and managers' attitudes, prejudices, and stereotypes about executive assistants and administrative professionals.

Joan is a passionate advocate for the administrative profession as a 'Career of Choice' and has dedicated her life to inspiring excellence and encouraging administrative professionals to reach for the stars. Joan is an accomplished author, professional speaker, coach, and corporate trainer. She has written five groundbreaking books for administrative professionals, an operating manual for executives and assistants, produced 350+ educational videos, designed 200+ educational programs, and coached 300+ executive/assistant teams.

Joan Burge and Office Dynamics' quest to provide extraordinary life- and career-changing educational programs, along with their passionate support of the administrative profession has earned the respect of elite clients including Walt Disney World, Cisco Systems, Caterpillar, Humana, and Procter & Gamble.